CONNEC~~T~~
Math & Li~~terat~~ure

Written by John and Patty Carratello

Illustrated by Blanca Apodaca, Cheryl Buhler,
Theresa Wright and Keith Vasconcelles

Teacher Created Materials, Inc.
P.O. Box 1040
Huntington Beach, CA 92647
©1991 Teacher Created Materials, Inc.
Made in U.S.A.

ISBN 1-55734-342-X

Table of Contents

Table of Contents *(cont.)*

Introduction

Connecting Math and Literature shows the classroom teacher how to use over forty high-quality literature selections to teach primary children such concepts as numbers, measurement, problem solving, and geometry. Children will love to read these books as they master these important math concepts.

Format

1.   Each literature selection is briefly summarized.

2.   Math concepts taught through the use of the book are identified.

3.   Activities that may be used to connect each book to math are suggested. Support materials for these activities are provided when necessary, including assessment tools and ideas.

4.   Activities that can extend the literature selections into the home and other curricular areas are suggested. Support materials for these activities are provided when necessary.

5.   A partial bibliography of math-oriented literature choices that are not mentioned in this book is included.

6.   An answer key for selected pages is provided.

In addition, we encourage you to use *Anno's Math Games* by Mitsumasa Anno (Philomel, 1982) as you plan your units. It provides an excellent introduction, reinforcement, enrichment, and review of the math concepts identified in *Connecting Math and Literature*.

We know you will enjoy teaching math through literature!

Counting Center

There is a glorious wealth of books that can be used to teach and reinforce counting skills in an enjoyable way. You may wish to develop a Counting Center in your classroom that will showcase these outstanding books as well as provide a place to display other counting-related materials. (*Sample Layout for Counting Center,* page 6)

Here are ideas for activities that can be done at your center:

- Supply numerous counting books that make counting fun. (*Some Great Counting Books,* page 7 and *Bibliography,* page 142)

- Encourage the use of math manipulatives for hands-on approach to learning about numbers. Some types of manipulatives you may want to include are beans, macaroni, unifix cubes, and number sticks. (*Now Serving Numbers!,* page 12 and *Number Sticks,* page 13)

- Provide numbers for the children to color and cut out for use when they create their own counting books. Kids love to make and share counting books! (*Numbers to Color,* page 8)

- Supply dot-to-dot puzzles in varying degrees of difficulty to develop and provide practice for reading and sequencing numbers. (*Dot-to-Dot Game,* page 9)

- Use manipulative and pattern puzzles to teach and reinforce odd-even knowledge. (*Odds and Evens,* page 10)

- Have a good supply of color-by-number activities to reinforce number recognition skills. (*Color by Number,* page 11)

- Encourage children to classify shapes and arrange them into sets. (*Shape Sets,* page 14 and 15)

- Introduce and reinforce the concept of greater than, less than, and equal to. (*Relationships Between Numbers,* page 16)

- Provide puzzles that help children match numerals with number words. (*Number Puzzles,* page 17)

- Anything else you think your children would enjoy as a counting activity.

Sample Layout for Counting Center

Counting Center

At this center you can:

• Select counting books to read
• Make colorful numerals
• Play counting games
• Arrange and count sets
• Solve number problems using symbols

Numbers to Color

Dot-to-Dot Games

Odds and Evens

Color by Number

Shape Sets

> Greater Than < Less Than = Equal To

1 to 10

One to Ten

1 to 10 by ones

5 to 50 by fives

10 to 100 by tens

Beans

Macaroni

Cubes

Crayons, Markers, Pencils

How Many Bugs in a Box?

1, 2, 3 to the Zoo

One Wooly Wombat

The Most Amazing Hide-and-Seek Counting Book

Anno's Counting Book

When Sheep Cannot Sleep

Bears on Wheels

Animal Numbers

Some Great Counting Books!

Here are just a few of the many great books you will want to include in your classroom Counting Center.

- *Anno's Counting Book* by Mitsumasa Anno
  Numbers, groups, and sets take place in a real setting in this book that shows the growth of a community.

- *Bears on Wheels* by Stan and Jan Berenstain
  Addition and subtraction are humorously presented as a bear on a unicycle encounters a variety of bears on and off their wheels.

- *1, 2, 3, To The Zoo* by Eric Carle
  Colorful and countable animals ride to their new home in the zoo.

- *How Many Bugs in a Box?* by David A. Carter
  Curious readers relish opening each box in this book to discover what kind of zany bug waits to be counted.

- *The Most Amazing Hide-and-Seek Counting Book* by Robert Crowther
  One hundred charming creatures and other things can be discovered and counted by sliding, pulling, and lifting the pages of this highly interactive counting book.

- *When Sheep Cannot Sleep* by Satoshi Kitamura
  What does a sheep count when he cannot sleep? Readers have to look at the pages very carefully to come up with the next number of things to be counted!

- *Animal Numbers* by Bert Kitchen
  Mothers and their babies are artistically arranged in and around numbers that tell how many baby animals to find.

- *One Wooly Wombat* by Rod Trinca and Kerry Argent
  The animals of Australia come forth to be counted in this colorful, educational counting book.

Numbers to Color

Color these numbers in an interesting way. Cut them
out and use them to make your own counting book!

1

2 3 4

5 6 7

8 9 10

Dot-to-Dot Game

9

Odds and Evens

Circle the odd numbers and draw a square around the even numbers.

| 1 | 4 | 9 | 12 | 16 | 21 | 25 |

| 28 | 33 | 35 | 38 | 41 | 46 | 50 |

1	2	3	4	5	6	7	8	9	10
11	12	13	14	15	16	17	18	19	20
21	22	23	24	25	26	27	28	29	30
31	32	33	34	35	36	37	38	39	40
41	42	43	44	45	46	47	48	49	50
51	52	53	54	55	56	57	58	59	60
61	62	63	64	65	66	67	68	69	70
71	72	73	74	75	76	77	78	79	80
81	82	83	84	85	86	87	88	89	90
91	92	93	94	95	96	97	98	99	100

Color all the even numbers red.

Color all the odd numbers blue.

Count to 40 using only even numbers.

2				12					
			28						40

Use the beans and macaroni at the Counting Center to count in sets from one to ten. Make all odd sets beans and all even sets macaroni. (1 bean, 2 pieces of macaroni, 3 beans, 4 pieces of macaroni, etc.)

Color by Number

Color this picture using the color key in the box.

1 = yellow	3 = blue	5 = green	7 = pink	9 = gray
2 = red	4 = orange	6 = purple	8 = brown	10 = black

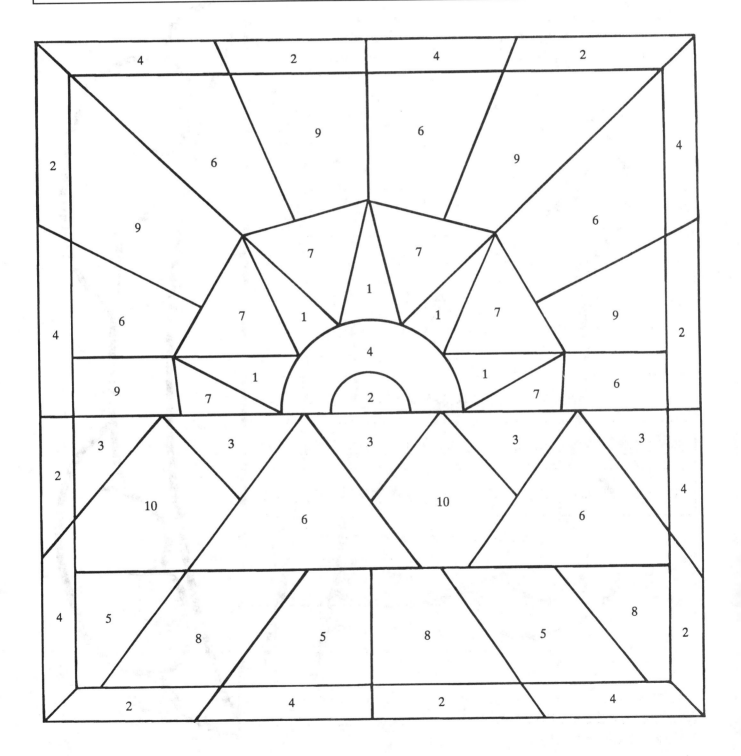

Now Serving Numbers!

- Enlarge this pattern to twice its size using an overhead projector. Duplicate or laminate the pattern on tag. Cut ten slits in the platter as shown. Put the bear on the Counting Center board.

- Students can put each group of *Number Sticks* in sequential order by poking the sticks through the slits on the serving platter.

Number Sticks

Color the squares 1-10 yellow. Color the squares 5-50 orange. Color the squares 10-100 green. Cut the numbers apart. Laminate them to increase their durability. Staple the numbers to the top of craft sticks. Put the finished number sticks in the Counting Center to be used with *Now Serving Numbers!*

1	2	3	4	5
6	7	8	9	10

5	10	15	20	25
30	35	40	45	50

10	20	30	40	50
60	70	80	90	100

Shape Sets

On these two *Shape Sets* pages, there are 55 shapes.
Here is what you will do with these shapes.

1. Color the shapes any colors you choose.
2. Carefully cut each shape out.
3. Arrange the shapes in shape sets of 1 to 10.
4. Glue or paste the shape sets on a
   large piece of construction paper.
5. Identify each shape set with
   its numeral and number word,
   as in the example to the right.

1   one

Shape Sets (cont.)

Use the shapes on this page to complete the activity described on page 14.

Relationships Between Numbers

For this center activity, you will use these symbols:

>	<	=
greater than	less than	equal to

Here is how to use the symbols to show relationships between numbers.

10 > 2	1 < 8	5 = 5
10 is greater than 2	1 is less than 8	5 is equal to 5

Fill in the correct symbol to show the relationship between each of the pairs of numbers below.

2 6 2 is less than 6	4 1 4 is greater than 1
100 100 100 is equal to 100	5 25 5 is less than 25
12 3 12 is greater than 3	47 62 47 is less than 62
21 40 21 is less than 40	51 52 51 is less than 52
75 37 75 is greater than 37	99 99 99 is equal to 99

Number Puzzles

Duplicate these number puzzles on tagboard. Cut them out. Place the numerals in the "1 to 10" pouch on the Counting Center. Place the number words in the "one to ten" pouch.

1	one	2	two
3	three	4	four
5	five	6	six
7	seven	8	eight
9	nine	10	ten

The Midnight Farm
by Reeve Lindbergh

At bedtime, a mother walks her young child around the farm to see the animals in the darkness. In this gentle and reassuring counting book, the sensitive mother helps her child understand that the darkness of night is a comfortable and safe place to be.

MATH CONCEPTS

• number   • comparison   • classifications   • sets

CONNECTING ACTIVITIES

• Review numbers one to ten. Be sure students can count things by using these numbers, as well as recognize and write the numerals and number words. (*Counting Center,* pages 5 to 17.)

• Give pairs of students piles of objects that can be sorted into different groups and counted into sets of one to ten. (For example, one pile of objects might consist of one straw, two pennies, three brads, four paper clips, five beans, etc.) When they have finished grouping, ask them to share why they grouped things the way they did.

• Introduce sets and relate them to *The Midnight Farm.* (*Sets,* page 19)

• Distribute *The Midnight Farm Animal Sets* (pages 20 to 23). Each complete set should be colored, cut out, labeled with the corresponding numeral, number word, and animal name, and arranged in numerical order. These sets can then be used for a variety of games, such as a memory game like "Concentration," a reading "Flash Card" game, or combined with other sets to play a "Go Fish" type of game. These sets are also great aids to help the students retell the story! Use the last set box as a tally form for counting the total number of animals grouped in sets in *The Midnight Farm.*

• Assess concept understanding. (*Do You Understand?*, page 24)

EXTENDING ACTIVITIES

• Ask students to retell *The Midnight Farm* to their families using their *Animal Sets* deck.

• Encourage students to look for sets all around them. Here are a few ideas:
  • sets in the kitchen   • sets in the backyard   • sets of favorite foods
  • sets in a toy box   • sets that are tiny   • things sold in sets

• Assign students to find and share sets of things, one to ten, that they have found at home.

• Encourage students to make their own "Deck of Sets" using their own illustrations or pictures from consumable magazines.

18

Sets

In *The Midnight Farm,* there are ten different groups of animals. Each of these different groups of animals is called a *set*. A *set* is a group of things that are alike in some way. Each animal in *The Midnight Farm* is put into a set because of the type of animal it is.

{ } is the sign that shows a set has been grouped together. Look at the sets on this page. Below each set, explain why the set members have been grouped together.

Midnight Farm Animal Sets

Use these sets of animals for the activities suggested on page 18.

Midnight Farm Animal Sets (cont.)

Use these sets of animals for the activities suggested on page 18.

Midnight Farm Animal Sets (cont.)

Use these sets of animals for the activities suggested on page 18.

There are _____ animals on the midnight farm.

____ dog   ____ cows

____ white cats   ____ sheep

____ raccoons   ____ chicks

____ geese   ____ deer

____ horses   ____ field mice

Numbers and Animals

Cut out these number and animal name cards and use them for *The Midnight Farm Animal Sets* activity described on page 18.

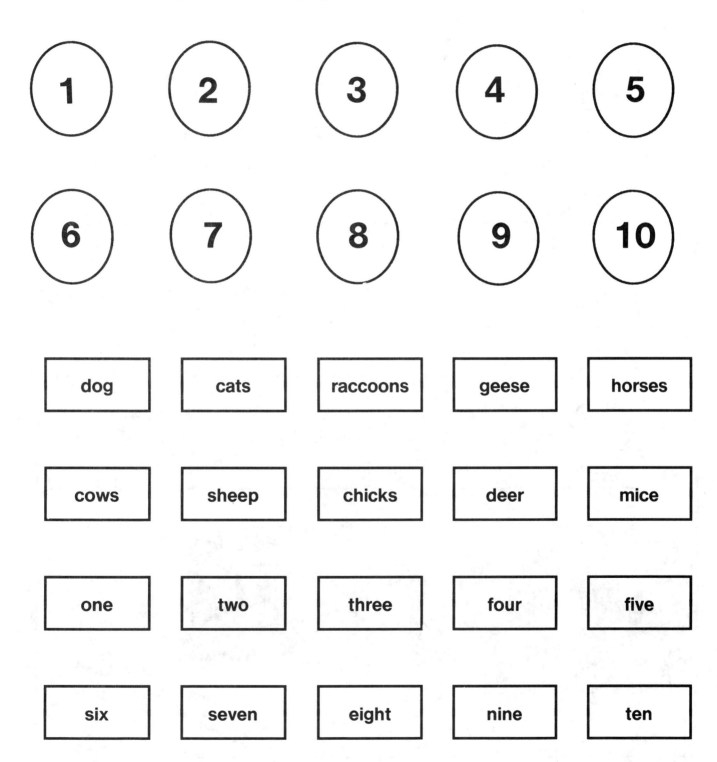

Do You Understand?

Draw the set sign { } around each group of things that can be put into a set because its members are alike in some way. Below each set, explain why the set members can be grouped together.

_____   _____

_____   _____

 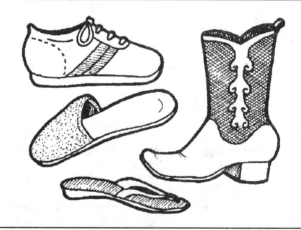

_____   _____

_____   _____

_____   _____

_____   _____

24

The Wolf's Chicken Stew

by Keiko Kasza

A very hungry wolf has a craving for some chicken stew. He spots a lone chicken, but decides to fatten her up a bit more first. During a three-night period, he anonymously provides her with food — 100 pancakes, 100 doughnuts, and a 100-pound cake. He is certain she is fattened up by now and goes to claim his prize. What he finds instead is a very grateful hen and her many (probably 100) chicks. He changes his mind about eating her, and plans her next gift — 100 cookies!

MATH CONCEPTS

- counting   • estimation   • measurement   • classification   • graphing

---

CONNECTING ACTIVITIES

- Ask the children to tell some of the wolf stories they know. Ask if the wolf in *The Wolf's Chicken Stew* is like most wolves in stories.

- The wolf in *The Wolf's Chicken Stew* loves to eat. Have students brainstorm the types of food they like to eat.

- Discuss how many 100 pancakes and 100 doughnuts would be. Practice counting, sorting, classifying, and graphing 100 things. Some things you might use are pattern blocks, unifix cubes, coins, crayons, or a picture filled with 100 things. (*100*, page 26)

- Discuss how much a 100-pound cake would be. Bring in objects or pictures of objects that weigh or add up to weigh 100 pounds.

- Celebrate the 100th Day at school with activities centered around the number 100. Groups can do these activities together, rotating through centers throughout the 100th Day. A few ideas you can use are found on page 27 and 28.

- Write dialogue that might have occurred if the wolf had caught the hen to eat *before* he tried to fatten her up, or if the wolf had confessed his true reasons for the food gifts to the hen.

- Assess concept understanding. Be sure all students can count to 100, can sort into groups that equal 100, and have an idea of how much 100 is in real-life situations.

EXTENDING ACTIVITIES

- Ask the students to bring 100 easily manageable things from home to share on the 100th Day. (baseball cards, marbles, stamps, toothpicks, hair clips, etc.)
- Give students ideas of things they can do at home to celebrate 100, such as:
  - Find the person in the family who is closest to 100 pounds.
  - Bounce a ball 100 times.
  - Think of something you like to do at home that takes 100 minutes.
  - Plan a normal-sized meal with 100 food items on the plate.
  - Build something with 100 pieces, like a block tower or puzzle.
  - Give someone in your family 100 hugs!

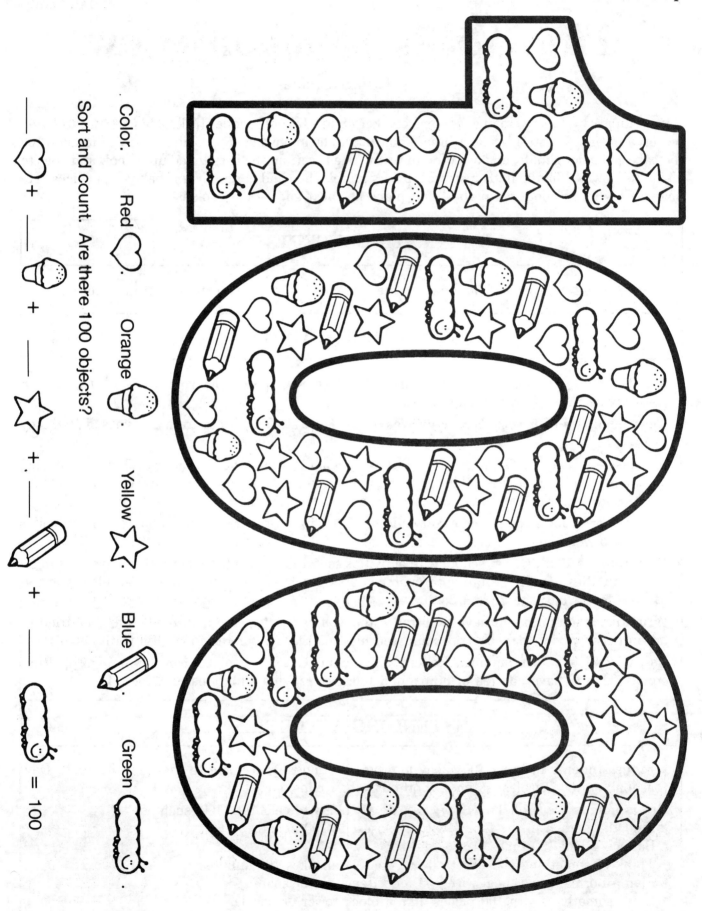

Sort and count. Are there 100 objects?

Color.   Red ♡ . Orange 🍦 . Yellow ☆ . Blue ✏ . Green 🐛 .

♡ + 🍦 + ☆ + ✏ + 🐛 = 100

100th Day Activity Cards

Cut apart these activity cards to use in centers on your 100th Day Celebration!

 Draw what you think you will look like when you are 100 years old.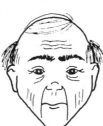

 Make a list of five things you have 100 of at home.

Estimate how far 100 steps would take you from where you are right now. Check your guess!

Which of these three jars has 100 beans in it? Mark your guess on the graph at this table.

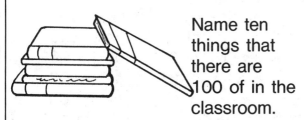 Name ten things that there are 100 of in the classroom.

 Count the 100 creatures or things that are pictured in one of the books on this table.

How many people do you think 100 kernels of unpopped popcorn can feed? After you make your guess, pop 100 kernels with adult supervision.

Could you eat 100 pancakes at one time? Name three things you *could* eat 100 of at one time!

100th Day Activity Cards (cont.)

Cut apart these activity cards to use in centers on your 100th Day Celebration!

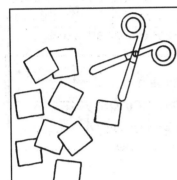 Figure out the fastest way for you and your group members to cut out 100 squares. Then, do it!

Work with your group to use the 100 squares you just cut out to make a picture.

 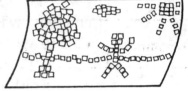

Count 100 M&M® candies. Sort them into sets by color. Then, graph the number of M&M®s in each color group on the graph at this table.

 Use a calendar to find out what month and date it will be 100 days from today.

 String a necklace of 100 Cheerios® or Fruit Loops® cereal. Wear it now, and eat it later for a snack!

Arrange unifix cubes (or other manipulatives) into:
- groups of 5 to make 100
- groups of 10 to make 100
- groups of 20 to make 100
- groups of 25 to make 100
- groups of 50 to make 100
- groups of 100 to make 100

Weigh yourself on this scale and write your weight on the paper at this table. Can you find two students in the classroom whose weight when added together is equal to 100 pounds?

Can you balance on one leg for 100 seconds? Use a partner with a stopwatch to time you.

How Much Is a Million?

by David M. Schwartz

Usually children have no realistic concept of how much a million is. In *How Much Is a Million?*, astronomical numbers like million, billion, and trillion are brought into focus by using things children can visualize. The facts will fascinate and the illustrations will delight readers of all ages!

MATH CONCEPTS

- number   • counting   • place value   • measurement   • comparison   • logic

CONNECTING ACTIVITIES

- Ask your students to explain the concepts of a million, a billion, and a trillion in any way they can.

- List things that the class members think they might be able to find a million, billion, or trillion of in school, at home, in the neighborhood, in town, or in the world.

- Discuss place value on a level that is appropriate for your students. (*What a Lot of Zeros!*, page 30)

- Find the average height of students in your class. How does it compare with the 4′8″ height the author used in the story?

- Test your students' understanding of large numbers and how they fit into "real" life with logic-oriented questions. (*What Do You Think?*, page 31)

- Ask your students if they counted each day in class, could they reach 1,000,000 by the end of the school year? Encourage explanations of their reasoning, including the length of school time each day that would have to be devoted to counting in order to reach the goal.

- Assess concept understanding. (*Do You Understand?*, page 32)

EXTENDING ACTIVITIES

- Make your own *How Much Is a Million?* books.

- Look for millions, billions, and trillions mentioned in books, magazines, and newspapers and listen for these numbers in conversations, radio, and television. Share what has been seen and heard in class. This will help make these large numbers more real for your students.

- Ask kids to explain astronomical numbers in everyday terms to their families.

- Start a "Million Jar" at home or school. Encourage students to collect one million of the same, small thing, like used postal stamps, bottle caps, or tiny pebbles. Don't get discouraged — it will take *quite* a long time! (Don't collect pennies. By the time you reach a million of them, they would have been better saved in a bank!)

What a Lot of Zeros!

Study this chart to learn about place value in very large numbers.

one trillions	one hundred billions	ten billions	one billions	one hundred millions	ten millions	one millions	one hundred thousands	ten thousands	one thousands	hundreds	tens	ones
1,	0	0	0,	0	0	0,	0	0	0,	0	0	0

Put the numbers in the box below in order from largest to smallest. Then, answer the questions.

10	1,000,000,000	100
1,000,000	1,000	1,000,000,000,000

_____ one trillion

_____ one billion

_____ one million

_____ one thousand

_____ one hundred

_____ ten

How many zeros are in:

one trillion? _____

one billion? _____

one million? _____

one thousand? _____

one hundred? _____

ten? _____

What Do You Think?

1. Without counting, how many stars do you think there are in this box? Circle your estimate.

   10   100   1,000   1,000,000

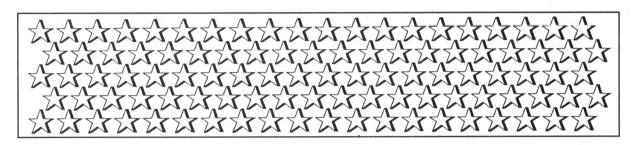

2. If you had a swimming pool large enough to hold a whale, what is the largest number of goldfish that could live in the pool (if the whale was out!)? Circle your answer.

   100   1,000   1,000,000   1,000,000,000   1,000,000,000,000

3. How many children would it take to cross your classroom floor, if they were lying head to heal on the floor. Circle your estimate.

   10   100   1,000   1,000,000

4. How many seconds do you think there are in one year? Circle your estimate.

Jan.	Feb.	Mar.
Apr.	May	June
July	Aug.	Sept.
Oct.	Nov.	Dec.

   hundreds   millions

   thousands   trillions

5. If you counted every day of your life, could you count to one billion? _____ Why?

   _____

   _____

6. If this 1,000,000 is a million, and
   this 1,000,000,000 is a billion, and
   this 1,000,000,000,000 is a trillion,
   What do you think a quadrillion would look like?

   _____

Do You Understand?

Match each number with its name.

1. _____ zero		a. 1,000
2. _____ one		b. 10
3. _____ ten		c. 1,000,000,000
4. _____ one hundred		d. 0
5. _____ one thousand		e. 100
6. _____ one million		f. 1,000,000,000,000
7. _____ one billion		g. 1
8. _____ one trillion		h. 1,000,000

Circle the things that can be measured in millions.

friends you have

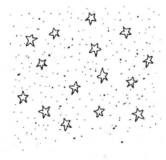
stars

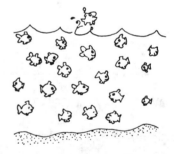
fish in the sea

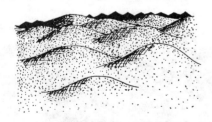
grains of sand

books you can read in a week

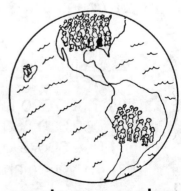
people on our planet

Annie's One to Ten

by Annie Owen

Not only is *Annie's One to Ten* a great counting book, it is a book that shows all the combinations of numbers that add up to ten. One rainbow and nine clouds, four cars and six motorcycles, and five ice cream cones and five birthday cakes are a few ways that show children how ten can look. Children, teachers, and parents will enjoy the colorful and entertaining way this book presents addition facts.

MATH CONCEPTS

- counting   - addition   - comparison   - storing   - classification   - sets

CONNECTING ACTIVITIES

- Arrange math manipulatives in as many combinations as possible that will equal ten. Require students to use manipulatives to make at least five different combinations of ten.

- Play a game in which ten students work as a group to arrange their bodies in different combinations of ten. The group then "performs" the number ten for the class as the class members call out the equation they see, such as "6+4=10" or "7+3=10."

- Teach number words as you read this book. (*Number Puzzles,* page 17)

- Look for sets of a similar nature in *Annie's One to Ten.* She has made her number combinations using related things, such as party things, foods, and vehicles.

- Divide the class into partners. Give each pair *Find the Tens!* (page 34 and 35.) Partners will work together to color the pictures, cut them out, arrange them into sets, and determine which sets can be added together to make ten.

- Assess concept understanding. (*Do You Understand?,* page 36)

EXTENDING ACTIVITIES

- Make counting books that show combinations of ten.

- Learn to count from one to ten in different languages.

- Use the book to show subtraction concepts as well.

- Encourage students to make combinations of ten at home for their families using toys, stuffed animals, silverware, or other things available to them. Ask parents to make combinations of ten for their children, too! Ask students to bring a combination of ten from home to share with the class. Be sure their choices are of a manageable size!

Find the Tens!

Work together to color these pictures and cut the squares out. Arrange the pictures into sets. Find the sets that can be added together to make ten.

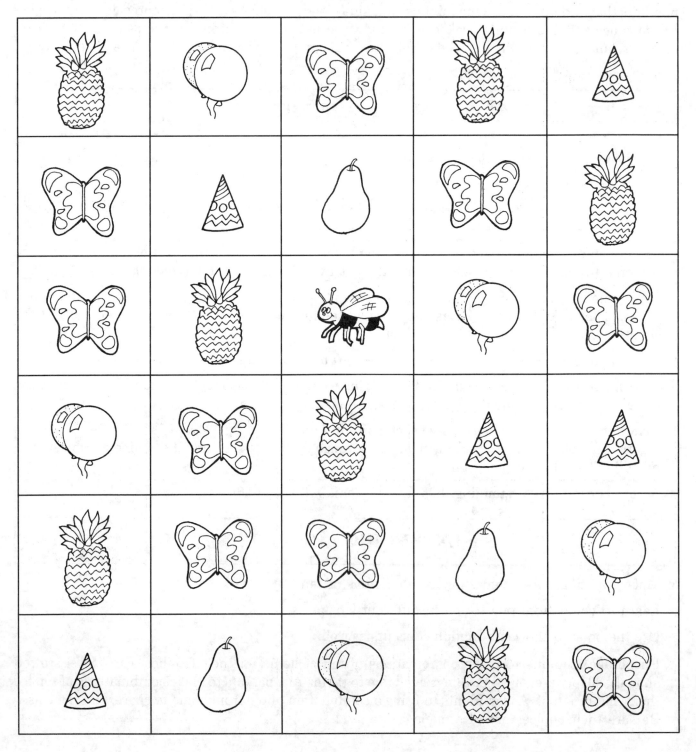

Find the Tens! (cont.)

Work together to color these pictures and cut the squares out. Arrange the pictures into sets. Find the sets that can be added together to make ten.

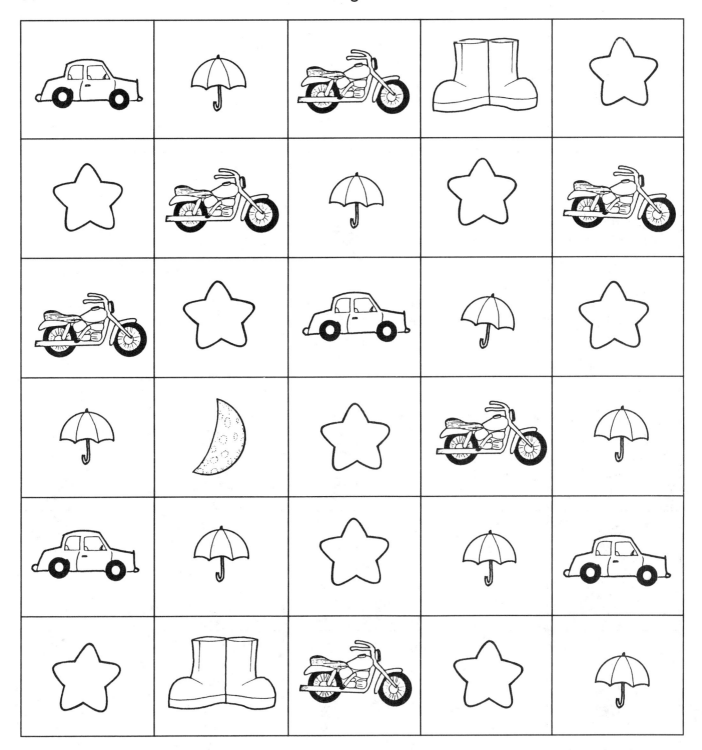

35

Do You Understand?

LEVEL 1

Color the shapes that have ten things inside them.

hearts and triangles

pencils and erasers

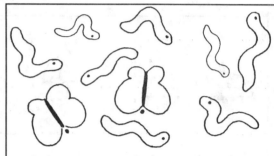

caterpillars and butterflies

shoes and hats

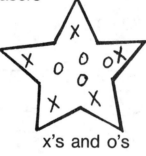

x's and o's

tulips and daisies

LEVEL 2

Add these numbers. Circle the combinations of things that equal ten.

3   +   5   =   _____   6   +   4   =   _____

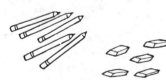

5   +   5   =   _____   5   +   4   =   _____

8   +   2   =   _____   2   +   3   =   _____

Ten Bears in My Bed

by Stan Mack

In this countdown book, ten bears have crowded into a small boy's bed and he wants them out. One by one they leave, in the most delightful ways!

MATH CONCEPTS

• number   • comparison   • patterns   • problem solving

CONNECTING ACTIVITIES

- Use manipulatives to tell the story, such as stuffed teddy bears in a bed made out of a box, or paper bears attached to a flannel board. Be sure to "costume" your bears appropriately!

- Ask children to sequence the bears in the order they left the story. (*Goodbye, Bears!,* page 38) They can use these bear pictures to retell the story.

- Practice subtraction skills using math manipulatives such as unifix cubes, pennies, cookies, paper clips, or counting bears.

- Make visual subtraction problems for the students to work out. (*Subtraction You Can See!,* page 39)

- Replace pictures of subtraction problems with numerals. (*Time for Numbers!,* page 40)

- Discuss the concept of none.

- Assess concept understanding by observing their skill level with ability-appropriate manipulatives, or written math equations.

EXTENDING ACTIVITIES

- Encourage the children to share some of the fantasies they have created that are like the fantasy created by the boy in the story.

- Make a vocabulary lesson out of the verbs that were used as the bears left the story.

- Brainstorm for other ways the bears could have left the little boy's room. Make a class book using ten of the verbs the students have suggested to replace the verbs Stan Mack used. Keep the same pattern for the class story, just change the verbs. Students can work in groups of two or three to complete each page.

- Have a "Teddy Bear Show." Kids can bring their own bears to share with the class.

- "Sing" the book!

Goodbye, Bears!

Color each of these bear pictures and cut them out. Put them in the order they left the boy's bed.

You can use these bear pictures to retell the story!

tootled out

pedaled out

galloped out

chugged out

flew out

rumbled out

roared out

jumped out

skated out

bounced out

Subtraction You Can See!

Complete the subtraction problems on this page. Then, if you would like, color the pictures!

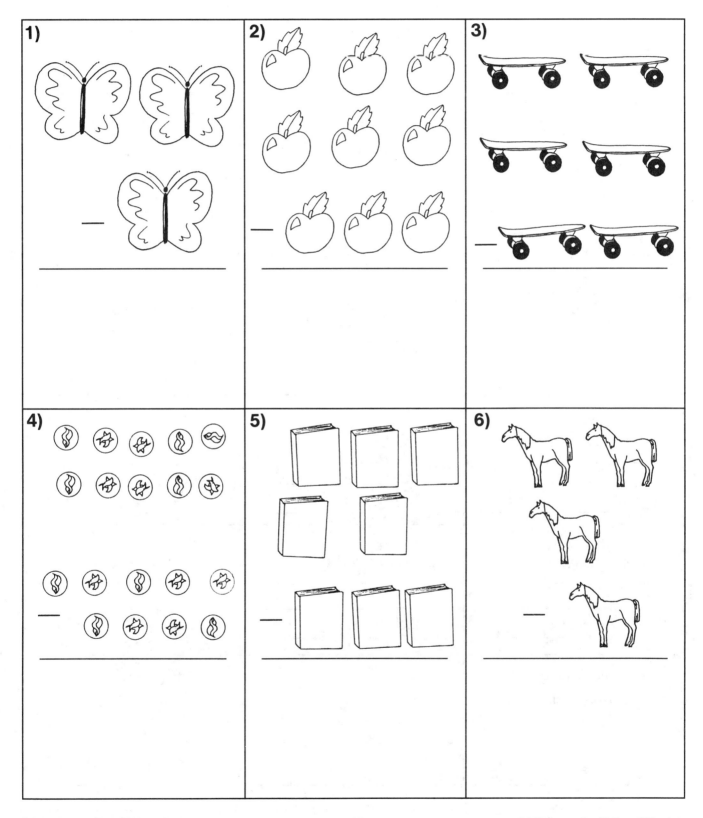

Time for Numbers!

Complete the subtraction problems on this page.

10 bears — 8 bears	9 cookies — 6 cookies	5 smiles — 4 smiles
7 teeth — 4 teeth	11 students — 1 student	8 grapes — 6 grapes
5 plates — 2 plates	3 dogs — 0 dogs	10 pencils — 4 pencils
9 toys — 5 toys	2 bicycles — 2 bicycles	4 friends — 2 friends
8 shoes — 4 shoes	12 eggs — 10 eggs	6 cars — 3 cars
4 baseballs — 3 baseballs	7 rocks — 1 rock	1 teacher — 0 teachers

Bunches and Bunches of Bunnies

by Louise Mathews

Bunnies multiply right before children's eyes as they read this colorful rhyming book. One hundred and forty-four charming bunnies entertain readers as they teach basic multiplication facts!

MATH CONCEPTS

* numbers   * operations   * multiplication   * capacity   * logic

CONNECTING ACTIVITIES

* As you read *Bunches and Bunches of Bunnies* to your students, reinforce the multiplication concepts shown in the book with math manipulatives such as unifix cubes, beans, or pennies.

* Invite students to manipulate small items to make the number combinations used in the story. Ask them to count their manipulatives carefully.

* After reading the story, and with your students' help, make 144 bunnies. Each student can make five or more bunnies and color each one differently. These bunnies can be used as manipulatives as the class retells the story to an audience. (*Bunny Pattern,* page 42)

* Match multiplication question cards with their answer cards. (*Match Them,* page 43)

* Investigate other combinations of numbers that can be multiplied to get the same totals. (*Many Ways To Get There!,* page 44)

* Assess concept understanding by testing the students' knowledge of multiplication facts with manipulatives or written problems.

EXTENDING ACTIVITIES

* Research to find out more about rabbits. If possible bring one (or more!) to class.

* As a class project, make a multiplication facts book like *Bunches and Bunches of Bunnies.*

* Make a list of rhyming words used in the story.

* Try some of the "acceptable" things mentioned in the book, such as planting seeds, learning dances, performing magic tricks, or having a parade.

* Discuss the concept of capacity as it relates to the number of bunnies a house could hold. Extend the capacity discussion to include other things that could hold bunnies and the capacity of each.

Bunny Pattern

Use this pattern to make the bunnies needed to retell *Bunches and Bunches of Bunnies.*

Match Them!

Cut these cards out.   Match each multiplication question card with its answer card.

(81 bunnies)	(25 bunnies)	(1 bunny)	$9 \times 9 =$	$5 \times 5 =$	$1 \times 1 =$
81	25	1			
(100 bunnies)	(36 bunnies)	(4 bunnies)	$10 \times 10 =$	$6 \times 6 =$	$2 \times 2 =$
100	36	4			
(121 bunnies)	(49 bunnies)	(9 bunnies)	$11 \times 11 =$	$7 \times 7 =$	$3 \times 3 =$
121	49	9			
(144 bunnies)	(64 bunnies)	(16 bunnies)	$12 \times 12 =$	$8 \times 8 =$	$4 \times 4 =$
144	64	16			

Many Ways To Get There!

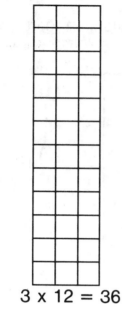

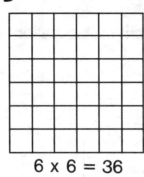

In *Bunches and Bunches of Bunnies,* six bunnies times six bunnies equals thirty-six bunnies. Here is how it looks in blocks.

6 x 6 = 36

There are other ways to multiply numbers to get thirty-six.

3 x 12 = 36

These blocks will show you how.

2 x 18 = 36

Here are some ways to multiply numbers to get twelve.

Can you find different ways to multiply numbers to get these totals?

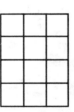

3 x 4 = 12

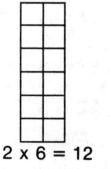

2 x 6 = 12

     16
          24
          30

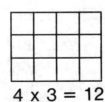

4 x 3 = 12

1 x 12 = 12

Use graph paper and crayons to help you!

1 x 36 = 36

Emma's Christmas

by Irene Trivas

In this book, a prince gives the young and beautiful Emma all the gifts that are mentioned in the song "The Twelve Days of Christmas" as many times as they are mentioned! It is a witty, delightful book that will provide your students with quite a number of things to multiply.

MATH CONCEPTS

- number   • sets   • operations   • addition   • multiplication   • patterns

---

CONNECTING ACTIVITIES

- Listen to the song "The Twelve Days of Christmas." Sing it as a class.

- As you read *Emma's Christmas*, keep a running tally of the types and numbers of gifts Emma receives each day. (*Emma's Gifts*, page 46) Use manipulatives to represent the gifts if that makes conceptualization easier for your students.

- Compute Emma's number of gifts by using both addition and multiplication skills. (*To Add or Multiply*, page 47)

- Discuss the prince's gifts in terms of sets. For example, you might ask your students how many were in the swan set. Or you may challenge their set-making skills by asking them to tell you the numbers in each of these sets: people, animals, plants, and things!

- Assess concept understanding by observing the students' ability to total the number of gifts that were given to Emma by the prince.

EXTENDING ACTIVITIES

- Discuss the characterizations of Emma, her mother, her father, and the prince. Are they realistic? Are they like people you know? Are their choices logical?

- Invite students to make their own gift lists of things they might give to someone special over a period of twelve days. Have them put their gifts into a song or story patterned after "The Twelve Days of Christmas."

- Learn more about the birds and people mentioned in *Emma's Christmas*.

- Write a new ending for the story.

- Describe the prince's gift to Emma on Christmas of the next year!

Record Emma's gifts on this chart.

Type of Gift	Day 1	Day 2	Day 3	Day 4	Day 5	Day 6	Day 7	Day 8	Day 9	Day 10	Day 11	Day 12	Total
Partridge in a Pear Tree													
Turtle Doves													
French Hens													
Calling Birds													
Golden Rings													
Swans Swimming													
Geese Laying													
Milkmaids Milking													
Pipers Piping													
Drummers Drumming													
Ladies Dancing													
Lords Leaping													

EMMA'S GIFTS

To Add or Multiply

Use both addition and multiplication skills to compute the number of gifts the prince gives Emma.

ADDITION													TOTAL
partridges	1	1	1	1	1	1	1	1	1	1	1	1	
turtle doves		2	2	2	2	2	2	2	2	2	2	2	
French hens			3	3	3	3	3	3	3	3	3	3	
calling birds				4	4	4	4	4	4	4	4	4	
golden rings					5	5	5	5	5	5	5	5	
swimming swans						6	6	6	6	6	6	6	
laying geese							7	7	7	7	7	7	
milking maids								8	8	8	8	8	
piping pipers									9	9	9	9	
drumming drummers										10	10	10	
dancing ladies											11	11	
leaping lords												12	

MULTIPLICATION									
gift	amount	X	days	total	gift	amount	X	days	total
partridges	1	x	12		laying geese	7	x	6	
turtle doves	2	x	11		milking maids	8	x	5	
French hens	3	x	10		piping pipers	9	x	4	
calling birds	4	x	9		drumming drummers	10	x	3	
golden rings	5	x	8		dancing ladies	11	x	2	
swimming swans	6	x	7		leaping lords	12	x	1	

The Doorbell Rang

by Pat Hutchins

As a mother offers her children a plate of cookies to share, the doorbell rings. Two neighbor children join them in the cookie-eating fun. But the doorbell continues to ring, bringing more and more children who are hungry for cookies. Soon, there are no more cookies left to share, and the doorbell rings. What will the children do?

MATH CONCEPTS

- number   • grouping   • addition   • division   • symbols   • logic

---

CONNECTING ACTIVITIES

- Practice counting skills. (*How Many?*, page 49)

- Color and cut out paper cookies to manipulate into combinations of twelve. (*A Dozen Cookies,* page 50 and *Share!,* page 51)

- After students have completed *Share!,* have them show at least six ways four people can share cookies. (3+2+4+3 or 1+6+2+3) Have them use *A Dozen Cookies* for manipulatives.

- Play *"The Doorbell Rang* Game." Choose twelve students to play the part of the children and students for the mother, grandmother, the doorbell, and the narrator. Dramatize the story, complete with real cookies! When you have finished, let the other half of the class perform the dramatization.

- Introduce the concept of division. (*Divide,* page 52) Have students practice dividing real things into two parts.

- Assess concept understanding. (*Do You Understand?*, page 54)

EXTENDING ACTIVITIES

- Bake cookies. Show how to double or half a recipe. When the cookies are ready to eat, you may choose to distribute them in a *The Doorbell Rang* way!

- Encourage students to look for sets of twelve at home. Show them how to divide twelve by two, three, and four. (*Twelve At Home,* page 53)

- Ask students to glue macaroni or beans on a page to show ten different ways to make twelve. Have them use + and = signs. (1+2+1+4+4=12 or 6+5+1=12 or 7+5=12, etc.)

How Many?

Write the number of cookies on each plate. Color the plate of cookies that will show how many cookies Ma made for Victoria and Sam.

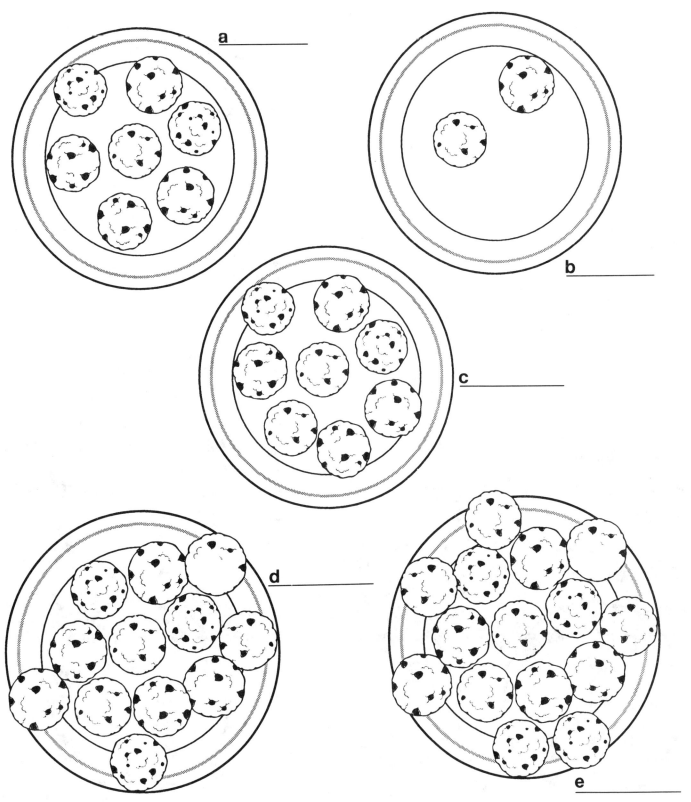

A Dozen Cookies

Color and cut out the cookies on this page.   Use these cookies for activities in this unit.

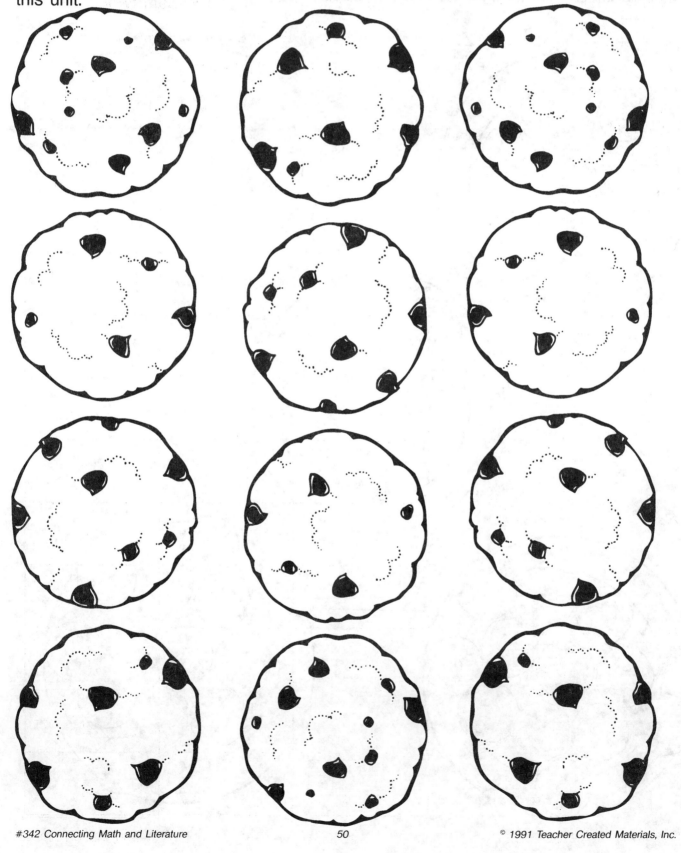

Share!

Ma told Victoria and Sam to share the cookies. They were not told to share the cookies equally, but they did. Victoria could have eaten ten and given Sam two!

How many ways can twelve cookies be shared between two people? Use the sets of cookies on page 50 to help you see how many ways Victoria and Sam could have shared the cookies.

Ways To Share Twelve Cookies		
Victoria	Sam	Total
		12
		12
		12
		12
		12
		12
		12
		12
		12
		12
		12

Divide!

Victoria and Sam wanted to share their cookies equally among their friends. They divided the cookies in such a way that no one person got any more than another.

When we divide things, we separate them into parts. Sometimes we divide by two. It is the same thing as dividing in half; ÷ is the symbol that shows that we divide.

Use your pencil to divide these things in two equal parts.

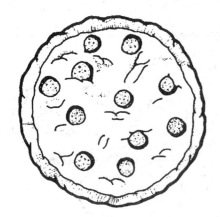

a pizza ÷ 2

a banana ÷ 2

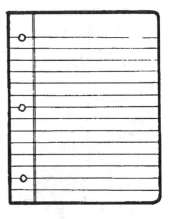

a piece of paper ÷ 2

4 children ÷ 2

6 shells ÷ 2

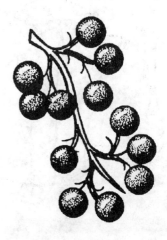

12 grapes ÷ 2

Twelve At Home

Victoria and Sam had a set of twelve cookies. They had to divide their cookies as new guests arrived.

Do you have sets of twelve in your home that you can divide? Here are some ideas. There are many more. Just look around!

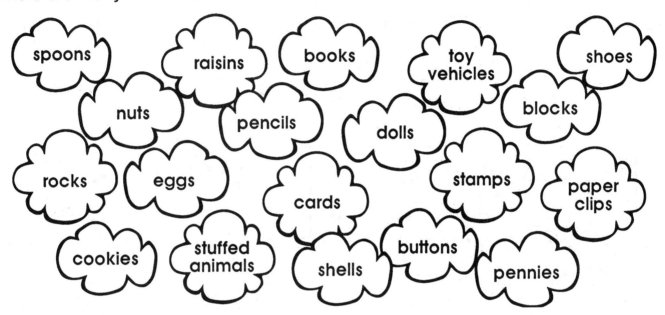

Choose a set from this list or a set idea of your own. Spread the set of twelve on a table or the floor. Practice dividing this set in halves, thirds, and fourths. Draw what your set divisions look like here.

Practice your division with other sets of twelve you can find at home.

Do You Understand?

Color the box that shows the symbol to divide.

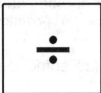  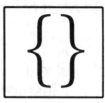 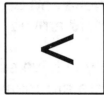

Draw how twelve cookies can be divided equally among the following groups of people.

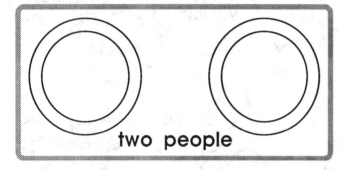

two people

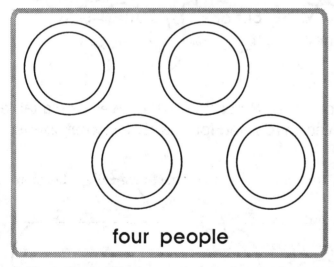

four people

six people

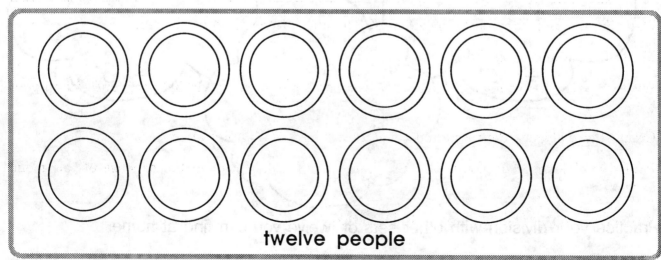

twelve people

Moira's Birthday

by Robert Munsch

Moira wants to have a birthday party and invite all of grade 1, grade 2, grade 3, grade 4, grade 5, grade 6, **and** kindergarten. And, without her parents' knowledge or consent, she does. What follows provides readers with a humorous look at estimation, problem solving, and patience!

MATH CONCEPTS

• number   • estimation   • measurement   • money   • problem solving

CONNECTING ACTIVITIES

• Estimate how many pizzas and cakes it would take to feed specific amounts of people. (*How Many?*, page 56)

• Ask students how many children came to Moira's party. Work with your students to determine how many children there would be if all the kids at *your* school in grades 1, 2, 3, 4, 5, 6, and kindergarten came to a party!

• Ask students how many children their parents would let them invite to a birthday party.

• Calculate the cost of 200 pizzas and 200 cakes.

• Practice dividing food into proportions that are adequate to feed specific numbers. (*We Can Feed You!*, page 57)

• Encourage students to share their opinions of Moira's methods for cleaning the house and getting rid of the extra food.

• Assess concept understanding by observing your students' ability to estimate logically. This is an on-going process!

EXTENDING ACTIVITIES

• Plan the ideal birthday party, including the number of people to be invited.

• Make a pizza and/or birthday cake.

• Write the dialogue you would have with *your* parents if you brought 200 party guests into your house.

• Create the dialogues the pizza and cake makers have with Moira and her parents.

• Plan a food menu that would feed 200 kids. If possible, calculate the expense of this menu as well.

• Write the story of Moira's next birthday party!

How Many?

Moira believed that she would need two hundred pizzas and two hundred birthday cakes to feed the two hundred guests she had invited to her birthday party.

Do you think the amount of pizzas and cakes she estimated she would need was too much, too little, or just right? Explain your answer.

_____

_____

_____

Now, it's your turn! Estimate how many pizzas and cakes you would need to feed each of these people or groups one slice of pizza and one piece of cake.

Person or Group	Number of Pizzas	Number of Cakes
you		
your family		
your class		
your grade		
your school		
the teachers at your school		
all your relatives		
your town		

Be ready to explain how you decided on the estimates you chose!

We Can Feed You!

Divide the pizzas so that the number of people in each box will all get an equal amount of pizza.

---

8 people

1. Divide these pizzas equally among eight people.

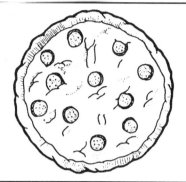 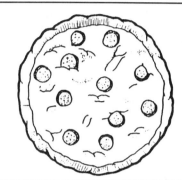

---

16 people

2. Divide these pizzas equally among sixteen people.

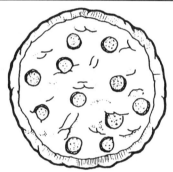 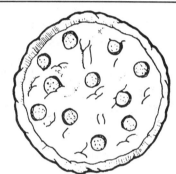

---

18 people

3. Divide these pizzas equally among eighteen people.

  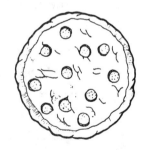

---

24 people

4. Divide these pizzas equally among twenty-four people.

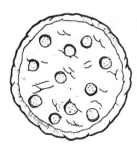 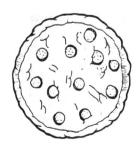 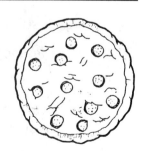

---

5. Work as a class to draw and divide enough pizzas for two hundred people!

Much Bigger Than Martin

by Steven Kellogg

Being the smaller and younger brother certainly has its disadvantages, especially for Henry. Martin makes him do all sorts of things he doesn't want to do, just because of his size. But Henry dreams of a different world, a world in which he is *Much Bigger Than Martin!*

MATH CONCEPTS

- measurement • size • comparison • numbers • symbols

CONNECTING ACTIVITIES

- Bring a sack of various items of different sizes. Pile them on a desk and compare them in pairs. Discuss the concepts of bigger than, smaller than, and equal to. (*Compare!*, page 59)

- Discuss the sorts of things Martin did to Henry to make him feel so badly about his smaller size. Encourage students to think of ways Martin could have made his brother feel better about himself. Ask students if they have had any similar experiences being the smaller or larger brother or sister.

- Introduce students to the symbols for greater than, less than, and equal to. (*Symbols,* page 60)

- Practice the use of >, <, and = . (*Use the Symbols,* page 61)

- Assess concept understanding. You may choose to make an assessment by watching students compare and classify manipulatives according to >, <, or = and/or by observing a successful completion of an activity such as *Use the Symbols!*

EXTENDING ACTIVITIES

- Discuss the realism of Henry's dreams.

- Encourage students to make those younger and smaller feel special.

- Present a lesson on overeating.

- Make a pair of stilts and try to walk on them.

- Draw a picture of one of Henry's dreams of being bigger than Martin. You may use an idea from the book or create a new dream for Henry!

- Brainstorm with the class for a list of things that can be done with friends, brothers, and sisters where size doesn't matter.

58

Compare!

Look at these block towers. See how they compare.

bigger than   smaller than   equal to

Color the object that is bigger in each set of two.

Color the object that is smaller in each set of two.

Color all the objects that are equal to each other in size.

Symbols

We use symbols to write math. Three symbols we can learn or review with the help of *Much Bigger Than Martin* are the symbols for greater than, less than, and equal to.

> greater than
< less than
= equal to

Martin's size is greater than Henry's size. Martin > Henry
Henry's size is less than Martin's size. Henry < Martin
In Henry's dreams, his size is greater than Martin's. Henry > Martin
When Martin was Henry's age, his size was the same as Henry's size. Martin = Henry

These faces will help you remember the symbols!

I'm bigger or greater. I'm always on the big side of the sign!

I'm smaller or less. I'm always on the small side of the sign.

Here I am, on the small side of the sign.

Here I am, on the big side of the sign!

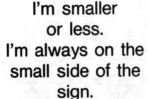

We're equal!

Use the Symbols!

Use the symbols for greater than (>), less than (<), and equal to (=) to complete these math equations.

Remember us!

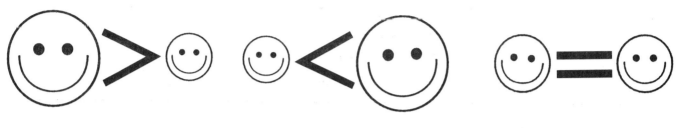

greater than   less than   equal to

1) 1 10	11) 9 5	21) 14 15
2) 4 2	12) 16 42	22) 74 74
3) 9 16	13) 37 37	23) 52 29
4) 5 5	14) 11 11	24) 12 0
5) 3 33	15) 0 6	25) 49 47
6) 10 9	16) 12 8	26) 93 93
7) 28 40	17) 51 50	27) 2 3
8) 64 64	18) 92 19	28) 31 27
9) 17 16	19) 10 10	29) 88 88
10) 0 0	20) 76 77	30) 5 4

Make three math equations of your own!

1) _____ 2) _____ 3) _____

Inch by Inch

by Leo Lionni

A quick-thinking inchworm saves his life by offering to measure the birds who want to eat him. Inch by inch, he measures the robin's tail, the flamingo's neck, the toucan's beak, the heron's legs, the pheasant's tail, and the hummingbird's body. But, when he agrees to measure the nightingale's song, he takes the opportunity to inch away to freedom!

MATH CONCEPTS

• measurement   • estimation   • comparison   • classification

CONNECTING ACTIVITIES

• Introduce the concept of a unit of measurement. (*Units,* page 63)

• Use an inchworm-filled picture to focus estimation skills. (*So Many Leaves!,* page 64)

• Estimate how many student body lengths it would take to measure large areas at school, such as the classroom width, the distance from the classroom door to the cafeteria, or the 50-yard dash. Then have the students lie head-to-heel and see!

• Introduce the concept of an inch. (*How Much Is An Inch?,* page 65)

• Determine what things can and can not be measured. (*YES or NO,* page 66)

• Measure specific things using an *Inchworm Ruler.* (*Inchworm Ruler,* page 67) Require students to keep a record of things they measure and their measurements.

• Assess concept understanding. (*Do You Understand?,* page 68)

EXTENDING ACTIVITIES

• Bring an inchworm to class. Watch it measure things! (An inchworm is the caterpillar larva of a geometrid moth.)

• Find out more about inchworms. Can they really measure things? How do they move? Do birds really eat them? What do they look like? Share the research findings in class.

• Determine what things in the home environment can be used to measure a length of paper. (*Units,* page 63) Share unit choices in class.

• Take *Inchworm Rulers* home to measure specific things. (*Inchworm Ruler,* page 67) Report things and their measurements in class.

• Make a list of things outside of the classroom that can and can not be measured in inches. Ask students to share and explain their classifications.

Units

The birds in *Inch by Inch* all had something they wanted measured. They had an inchworm do the measuring for them, using his body length as one unit of measurement.

Many things can be used as units of measurement. Just look at this page! Its length is:

- over 4 snap-together blocks

- almost 2 toothbrushes

- about 2 pencils

- close to eight pieces of pasta

- more than 10 nickels

- nearly 9 inchworms

Take this paper home. Find 10 different things in your house or yard that you can use as units of measurement to measure the length of this paper. Draw or write your units of measurement on the back of this paper.

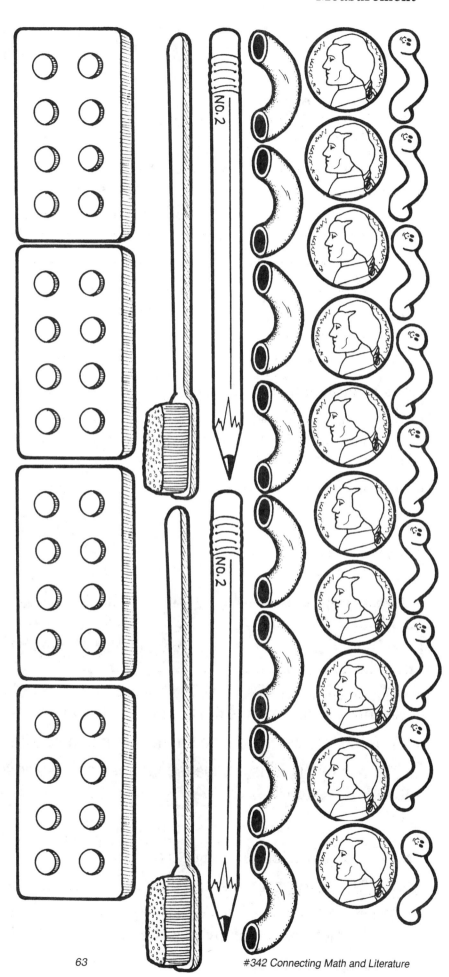

So Many Leaves!

Each of these inchworms has a leaf to measure.

1. Which inchworm has the longest leaf to measure? _____

2. Which inchworm has the shortest leaf to measure? _____

3. Which two worms are measuring the same-sized leaf?

   _____ and _____

4. Which inchworm will finish measuring first? _____

5. Which leaf is longer — Sue's or Judy's? _____

6. If they both go the same speed, will Joey or Sue finish measuring the leaf first?

   _____

Color the picture. In *Inch by Inch*, Leo Lionni made his inchworm emerald green.

How Much Is An Inch?

We live in a world where things are measured. We are measured from the time we are born and as we grow. We measure things around us all our lives.

The birds in *Inch by Inch* wanted to be measured. The inchworm measured them in inches.

How much is an inch? Color the inchworm on the leaf that you think is an inch long.

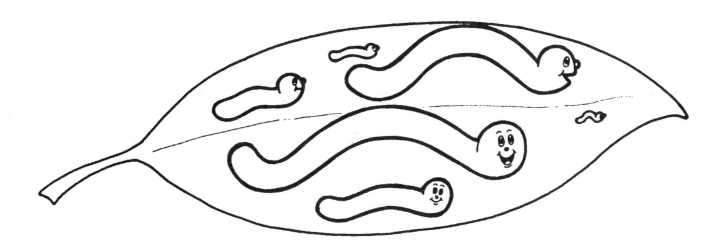

Unfold this paper to check your guess!

- -

This ⬭ is an inch-long inchworm! Using this inchworm as a measure, how many inches are the following things?

a pencil

_____ inches

a finger

_____ inches

a paperclip

_____ inch

YES or NO

Read each of the bubbles on this page. Decide if the things in these bubbles can or can not be measured in inches. If something can be measured, use green to color the bubble and one "YES" box on the graph at the bottom of this page. If it can not be measured, use yellow to color the bubble and one "NO" box on the graph. Then, answer the questions below the graph.

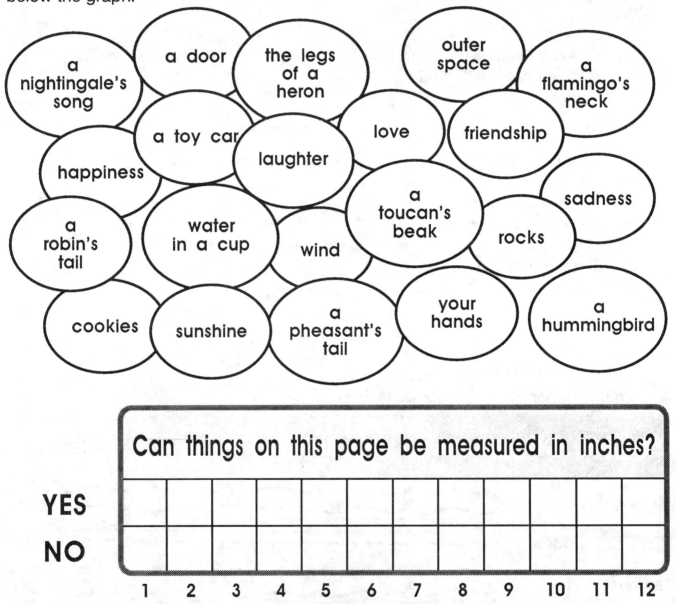

1. How many things on this page can be measured in inches? _____
2. How many things on this page can not be measured in inches? _____
3. Are there more things on this page that can be measured or that can not be measured in inches? _____ How many more? _____

Inchworm Ruler

Note: Duplicate on heavy paper.

Directions:

- Color the inchworm ruler pieces.

- Cut them out.

- Glue the two parts together.

- Name your inchworm. Write the name you choose on the inchworm's body.

- Use your Inchworm Ruler to measure things!

Do You Understand?

Color the things in this box that can be *easily* used to measure this paper's length.

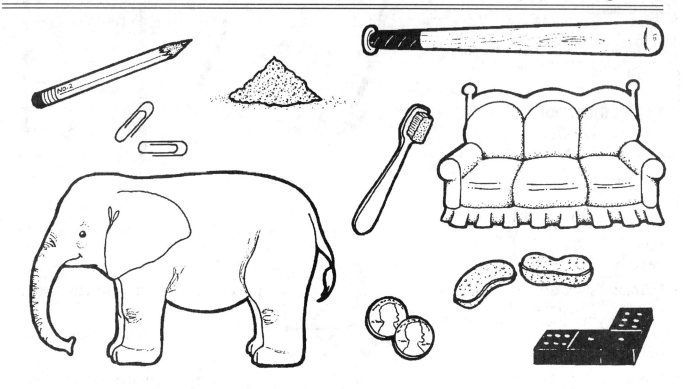

Color the inchworm that is an inch long.

Write a list of ten things that can be measured in inches.

1. _____
2. _____
3. _____
4. _____
5. _____

6. _____
7. _____
8. _____
9. _____
10. _____

Who Sank the Boat?

by Pamela Allen

Five animal friends set out one day to go for a ride in a rowboat. But, one of the friends sank the boat. Readers are invited to guess if it was a cow, a donkey, a sheep, a pig, or a mouse who did the sinking. They will be surprised when they find the answer at the end of the book!

MATH CONCEPTS

- measurement
- mass
- comparison
- estimation
- graphing
- sets

CONNECTING ACTIVITIES

- Make a pile of a combination of light and heavy things on a desk in the classroom. Ask students to **make two sets** out of the pile. In one set will be all the light things, in the other set, the heavy things.

- Introduce or review the concepts of ounce, pound, gram, and kilogram. Discuss the mass of an object as determined by its weight.

- Ask students to put objects in order from lightest to heaviest by an estimation of their weight. (*Order Us!*, page 70) Check for accuracy with a scale in class.

- Use a small toy boat and small objects to dramatize the story, calling your dramatization *"What Sank the Boat?"* Float the boat in a small tub of water as the students gradually add things like erasers, paper clips, nickels, and other small items.

- Let students practice using scales.

- Estimate the weights of ten *willing* volunteers as a class. Arrange them in order of lightest to heaviest, according to class opinion. Then weigh them and graph their weights. (*Graph the Weights!*, page 71)

- Bend a paperclip so that it can hold a number of other paperclips on its "hook." Suspend the unbent end from a magnet. Ask students to guess how many paperclips the magnet can hold. Then, try it!

- Assess concept understanding by having students order five objects from lightest to heaviest using their estimation skills. Then, they must be able to weigh the objects to determine the accuracy of their guesses.

EXTENDING ACTIVITIES

- Ask students to find something at home that is small and heavy and something that is large and light. When these objects have been brought to class, use them for mass estimation games!

- Create the story of the *second* rowboat ride of the characters in *Who Sank the Boat?*

- Discuss the reasons why the mouse sank the boat.

Order Us!

Color the pictures in the boxes below and cut each box out. Determine what you think are the lightest and heaviest things. Then, arrange all the cards in order from lightest to heaviest, according to your estimation.

You can check the accuracy of your estimation in class by weighing the objects on a scale!

a can of soup	a marble	a feather
a pencil	an apple	a basketball
a penny	a stick of gum	this book

Graph the Weights!

Select ten people from your class who would like to have their weights graphed in class. Write the name of each person and the person's weight on these lines.

1 _____ _____   6 _____ _____

2 _____ _____   7 _____ _____

3 _____ _____   8 _____ _____

4 _____ _____   9 _____ _____

5 _____ _____   10 _____ _____

Enter the names and weights on the graph below.

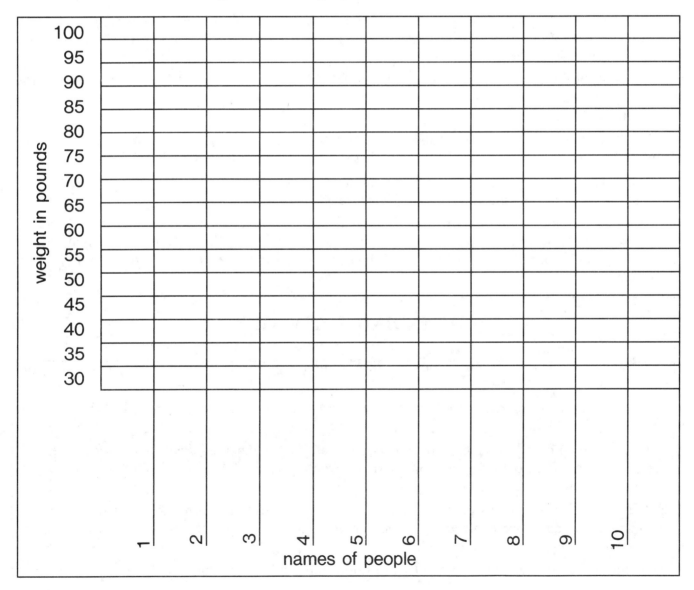

The Giant Jam Sandwich

by John Vernon Lord

A village plagued by four million wasps came up with an unusual plan for ridding their town of the pesty nuisance. They made a giant jam sandwich, and trapped the hungry insects inside!

MATH CONCEPTS

- measurement • capacity • large numbers • estimation

CONNECTING ACTIVITIES

- Write "four million wasps" on the board. Discuss the concept of how much four million would be. *How Much Is A Million?* by David M. Schwartz is a book that is very helpful for understanding the quantity involved in large numbers.

- Experiment with various things (popcorn, beans, pennies, etc.) to fill containers. Ask students to estimate how many things it will take for a container to be filled. (*How Much in a Cup?,* page 73) Talk about capacity.

- Bring "Guessing Jars" to class. Allow every student a chance to write down an estimate of the number of things in a jar. The student with the closest guess wins a prize!

- Ask students to estimate how many wasps (and other creatures) would be attracted to a realistically-sized jam sandwich. (*How Many?,* page 74)

- Assess concept understanding. Be sure each child can demonstrate an understanding of capacity by: estimating how many of one thing can fill a container; filling the container with that thing; counting the number of things it took to fill the container; and comparing the total with his or her estimation.

EXTENDING ACTIVITIES

- Ask students to make their own "Guessing Jars" at home and bring them to school to stump their classmates!

- Research wasps. Be sure to find out if they ever travel in large groups and what they like to eat.

- Read a recipe for bread, and look at the size of one loaf. Try to imagine (or calculate!) the amount of ingredients necessary to make a loaf of bread that would fill a refrigerator, fill a bedroom, and fill a building like the one used to bake bread in the story.

- Pose this problem for your students. "The next summer in Itching Down, no wasps came to live. Instead, the villagers were plagued by four million rats! How did the people of the town rid themselves of this new nuisance?"

- Ask students if a story like *The Giant Jam Sandwich* could really happen.

How Much in a Cup?

In this activity, children working in small groups estimate the capacity of various-sized cups for specific things.

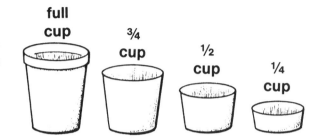

- 4 same-sized picnic cups for each group, cut to the proportions shown on the right.

- ability-appropriate "fillers"

   The things you choose to fill the cups must be appropriate to the counting skills of your class. For example, a half-cup of uncooked rice grains would be too frustrating for "new" counters to count, but a half-cup of marbles or *cooked* popcorn would be reasonable.

Here are some suggested fillers.

- popcorn (cooked or uncooked)
- bottle caps
- seedpods
- lentils

- paperclips
- pennies
- marbles
- buttons
- erasers
- peanuts

- jelly beans
- dry beans
- cereal circles
- grapes
- brads
- checkers

- uncooked macaroni
- rocks
- marshmallows
- beads
- rubber bands

Divide children into groups of two or three. Give each group four differently-sized cups filled with appropriately chosen things. The group then estimates how many things are in each cup and writes their guess on paper. They *may not* adjust their guesses! The group members count the items in each cup to determine the accuracy of their guesses. Encourage the children to talk about what they discovered!

How Many?

There is one half of a jam sandwich on this page. How many of each of the following things do you think it could catch? After you have made your estimates, discuss your answers in class.

wasps _____   grasshoppers _____   mice _____

ants _____   butterflies _____   bees _____

spiders _____   crickets _____   fleas _____

butterfly

mouse

bee

ant

flea

spider

grasshopper

wasp

cricket

A Circle of Seasons

by Myra Cohn Livingston

The vivid images of poetry capture the essence of each of the four seasons and bring them to life in *A Circle of Seasons*. Spring, summer, autumn, and winter delight the readers with their distinctive personalities. Even the youngest children who hear or read this book will remember how spring "Sticks a straw of sunshine down and whispers words to grow:

> O seed
> And root,
> Send forth a tiny shoot!"

MATH CONCEPTS

- measurement   • time   • classifications   • comparison   • sets

CONNECTING ACTIVITIES

- Ask students to explain the seasons *before* you read *A Circle of Seasons*.

- Discuss the cycle of the seasons.

- Paint pictures of each season.

- Discuss the meaning of each of the stanzas of poetry in *A Circle of Seasons*.

- Make sets of things that are characteristic of each season. (*Season Sets*, pages 76 and 77)

- Classify works from *A Circle of Seasons* into seasonal groups. (*Classify!*, page 78)

- Assess concept understanding. (*Do You Understand?*, page 79)

EXTENDING ACTIVITIES

- Sing seasonal songs.

- Discuss why there are seasons.

- "Adopt" a tree and study the changes it undergoes throughout the year.

- Encourage students to make lists with their families about the things they like about each season.

- Create a play or a dance about the seasons and perform it!

Season Sets

Color each of the pictures on this page. Then, cut out each of the boxes and combine them with the boxes you have cut from page 77. Group the pictures into **season sets**, putting all spring things together, all summer things together, all autumn things together, and all winter things together. Be ready to explain why you grouped the sets the way you did!

plum, peach, cherries

snowman

baby birds in a nest

Jack-o-lantern

snowcap, muffler, and mittens

a green sprout breaking through the snow

Season Sets (cont.)

Color each of the pictures on this page. Then, cut out each of the boxes and combine them with the boxes you have cut from page 76. Group the pictures into season sets.

sled

swimming pool

hot weather

squirrel collecting acorns

falling, colorful leaves

budding flowers

Classify!

Classify the words on this page into seasonal groups by writing them under the appropriate season on the classification chart below. If you need some help, reread *A Circle of Seasons*. These words all came from the book!

green buds	freezing	gold pumpkins	sizzle
purple plum	snowflake	blizzard	fragrant
acorns	harvest	blasts	blazing
ice crystals	warm rain	tiny shoot	yellow leaves

WORDS OF THE SEASONS

Spring 	Summer 
_____	_____
_____	_____
_____	_____
_____	_____

Autumn	Winter
_____	_____
_____	_____
_____	_____

Do You Understand?

Color the pictures that belong in the seasonal boxes below. Do not color the picture if it is in the wrong box! Then, cut each box out and arrange the boxes in the order they happen in nature. Glue your "circle of seasons" on a strip of contruction paper.

The Year At Maple Hill Farm

by Alice and Martin Provensen

Each month of the year brings a different scene to a farm in the country. Through pictures and words, readers discover what is unique to the months as they watch the year pass at Maple Hill Farm.

MATH CONCEPTS

- measurement   • time   • classifications   • sets   • sequence

CONNECTING ACTIVITIES

- Chart the number of student birthdays in each month of the year. (*A Year of Birthdays!*, page 81)
- Sing month sequencing songs.
- Discuss the concept of a month.
- Compare and contrast the qualities of the months of the year in your town and Maple Hill Farm. Discuss what is unique about each month.
- Practice reading, spelling, and capitalizing month names. (*Month Fun!*, page 82)
- Ask students to name something the animals on Maple Hill Farm do each month. Ask them something they do that is different for each month.
- Ask students to choose their favorite month and explain why it is their favorite.
- Arrange the months of the year in seasonal sets. (*Month Fun!*, page 82)
- Collect outdated calendars. Have students use the pictures from these calendars and other picture sources to create monthly bulletin board displays.
- Assess concept understanding. (*Do You Understand?*, page 83)

EXTENDING ACTIVITIES

- Visit a farm and see the animals. If possible, visit the farm more than once a year so students can see the changes about which Alice and Martin Provensen have written.
- Keep a log of a pet's changes throughout the year. Does your cat have less hair in the month of July? Is your dog energetic in October? Share observations with the class.
- Encourage students to make their own calendars, choosing pictures from magazines or their own artwork to convey the specialness of each month. A calendar blank can be found on page 86.
- Honor each month as it passes with a "Goodbye Celebration." Students can share what has been special about each month. Welcome new months as well, asking students to share what they are eagerly anticipating!
- Research the history of the names of the month.
- Ask students to compile a list of the special things they do with their family that are month-related. Have them share their lists with the class.

A Year of Birthdays!

Use an overhead projector to enlarge this page to a size that would be appropriate for your classroom use. Make a drawing of the projection, color it, and cut it out. Ask your students to write their names on the chart next to their birthday month. Add your name, too!

A YEAR OF BIRTHDAYS!

Month	Student Names	Birthday Totals
January		
February		
March		
April		
May		
June		
July		
August		
September		
October		
November		
December		

Month Fun!

Hunt for the names of the months in this wordsearch puzzle. Circle the months as you find them.

W	S	D	E	C	E	M	B	E	R	B	E	T	S	A	E
D	S	A	A	U	H	W	D	R	E	N	S	E	G	Y	J
D	E	Z	G	H	G	S	E	T	J	P	H	G	B	V	A
F	G	X	K	J	F	E	B	R	U	A	R	Y	M	F	N
V	N	O	I	W	K	H	U	L	N	P	O	P	K	E	U
M	M	M	A	Y	S	G	T	S	E	R	N	B	O	S	A
U	W	A	B	P	Z	C	S	Z	K	I	C	M	A	G	R
A	Z	R	H	L	A	A	E	Q	D	L	A	J	U	L	Y
Q	A	C	J	Y	B	P	P	A	Z	D	Z	E	G	O	D
Z	W	H	P	V	O	C	T	O	B	E	R	G	U	P	J
S	X	T	W	C	J	D	E	K	E	U	I	F	S	L	H
E	D	J	N	O	V	E	M	B	E	R	T	S	T	K	T
C	R	G	E	A	D	H	B	E	Y	Q	E	P	E	J	E
F	V	F	Q	X	S	J	E	W	U	J	S	K	W	U	Q
T	E	C	Z	E	W	L	R	R	I	P	C	L	Q	T	E

January   July
February   August
March   September
April   October
May   November
June   December

Write the names of the months in order in the seasons where they belong.

Winter	Spring	Summer	Autumn

Match something that happens at Maple Hill Farm with the month it happens in.

1. ____ Eggs are being laid by birds everywhere.   a. March
2. ____ The food on the farm has been harvested.   b. June
3. ____ Insects are all over!   c. April
4. ____ These days are hot and lazy.   d. August
5. ____ Animals give birth to babies.   e. May
6. ____ Animals begin to lose their winter fur and feathers.   f. October
7. ____ Wild deer look for apples under the snow.   g. November
8. ____ The first thin ice is beginning to form on the pond   h. January
         at the farm.

Do You Understand?

Rewrite the names of the months of the year in the right order. Then, circle all spring months in green, all summer months in red, all autumn months in orange, and all winter months in blue.

June	January	December	July
April	October	February	March
November	August	May	September

1. _____   7. _____

2. _____   8. _____

3. _____   9. _____

4. _____   10. _____

5. _____   11. _____

6. _____   12. _____

Choose two months from the twelve months of the year. Draw a picture or write a description about something that is special about each of the months you chose.

month: _____   month: _____

The Very Hungry Caterpillar

by Eric Carle

This colorful book follows the life cycle of a very hungry caterpillar, who is born on Sunday, eats gloriously Monday through Saturday, and transforms into a spectacular butterfly on the next Sunday. Children who read this book can practice counting skills, sequence the days of the week, and learn more about the life cycle and food choices of an engaging little bug!

MATH CONCEPTS

- measurement • time • counting • sequence • graphing • logic • sets

CONNECTING ACTIVITIES

- Ask students to name (or read, spell, and/or write) the days of the week in sequential order.
- Discuss the concept of a day and a week, and how they relate to a month, a season, and a year.
- Sing songs that sequence the days of the week.
- Match the food sets the hungry caterpillar ate with the correct dining day. Discuss the food choices made by the caterpillar. (*What A Hungry Little Guy!,* page 85)
- Practice calendar reading skills. Fill in the dates of the current month on the *Calendar Blank,* page 86. Then, ask your students day and date-related questions such as "What day of the week is March 31?" or "What day and date is exactly two weeks from September 16?"
- Assess concept understanding by asking the students to sequence the days of the week at a level appropriate to their ability (verbal or written). Ask them also to name some of the amounts and types of food the hungry caterpillar ate.

EXTENDING ACTIVITIES

- Research and discuss the life cycle of a caterpillar, including the length of time it takes for an egg to develop into a butterfly!
- Discuss food groups and the nutritional value of different types of food mentioned in *The Very Hungry Caterpillar.*
- Make lists of the types of food you would like to stuff yourself with!
- Find a caterpillar and put him safely in a terrarium. Offer him various food choices and record the amounts and types of food he ate daily.
- Ask students to make at least one meal for their family.
- Encourage students to make their own days-of-the-week books.
- Use the *Calendar Blank,* page 86, to record one thing each day that the class determines has been, is, or will be special.
- Create a caterpillar and a butterfly using available art supplies.

What a Hungry Little Guy!

Match the food sets the hungry caterpillar ate with the correct dining day.

1. ____ four strawberries

2. ____ one apple

3. ____ three plums

4. ____ one piece of chocolate cake, one ice-cream cone, one pickle, one slice of Swiss cheese, one slice of salami, one lollipop, one piece of cherry pie, one sausage, one cupcake, and one slice of watermelon

5. ____ two pears

6. ____ one nice green leaf

7. ____ five oranges

a. Monday

b. Tuesday

c. Wednesday

d. Thursday

e. Friday

f. Saturday

g. Sunday

Circle the foods mentioned above that might be on a real caterpillar's diet. Cross out the foods that you think a caterpillar would probably never get a chance to taste in real life.

Calendar Blank

| | | | | | Sunday |
					Monday
					Tuesday
					Wednesday
					Thursday
					Friday
					Saturday

The Grouchy Ladybug

by Eric Carle

Angrily leaving a leaf full of aphids that it did not want to share with another ladybug, the grouchy ladybug flew off in search of a fight. Each hour of the day it encountered an opponent that it felt was just "not big enough" to fight. By the end of the day, the grouchy ladybug was ready to challenge a whale. But the whale, with a slap of his tail, sent the ladybug back toward land. Wet, hungry, and tired, the grouchy ladybug once again was offered the chance to share aphids with the friendly ladybug. This time, the offer was graciously accepted!

MATH CONCEPTS

- measurement • time • counting • sequence • estimation • comparison • fractions

---

CONNECTING ACTIVITIES

- Dramatize the story with the children playing the parts of all the animals.
- Discuss the importance of sharing.
- Introduce or review the concepts of seconds, minutes, and hours. Play time-estimating games related to seconds, minutes, and hours to make time concepts real for the children. (*How Long Does It Take?*, page 88)
- Instruct students in time-telling skills. Include a discussion of the second hand, the minute hand, and the hour hand.
- Practice the placement of the numbers in the correct positions on the clock face.
- Make *Ladybug Clocks,* page 89. Encourage students to pair up for telling time practice, each partner using his or her own clock to "quiz" the other partner in telling time skills.
- Teach students how to divide the clock into halves and quarters to learn how to tell half hour and quarter hour times.
- Present size-comparison concepts, such as bigger than, smaller than, and equal to, as they relate to the ladybug and the other creatures in *The Grouchy Ladybug.*
- Assess concept understanding. (*Do You Understand?*, page 90) This page may also be used throughout the unit for a telling time practice paper. Depending upon which is appropriate for the level of your students, draw the picture or write the word which identifies each of the times you want your students to learn. Ask students to complete the page, either by drawing the minute and hour hands above the written time, or by writing the time below the correctly drawn time. For the final assessment, use the times mentioned in *The Grouchy Ladybug.*

EXTENDING ACTIVITIES

- Retell the story of the grouchy ladybug in class, with students using their *Ladybug Clocks* to make each time as you read it. Ask them to take their clocks home to help them retell the story to their families.
- Research the ladybug's role as a garden helper.
- Discuss aggressive behavior and its consequences.
- Discuss the importance of the ability to tell time.
- Brainstorm for ideas of what would happen if there were no clocks anywhere in the world.

How Long Does It Take?

Decide how each of the things in the questions below can be measured most accurately in seconds, minutes, or hours. Write your answer on the blank next to each question. When you have finished, compare your time ideas with others in class or at home.

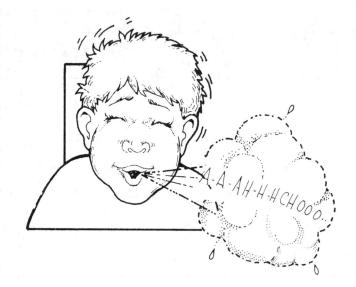

1. How long does it take to sneeze?

   _____
2. How long does it take to eat lunch at school? _____
3. How long does it take to brush your teeth? _____
4. How long does it take your mother or father to shop for food? _____
5. How long does it take to draw a really nice picture? _____
6. How long does it take to play outdoors with a good friend? _____
7. How long does it take for you to fall asleep once you are in bed for the night? _____

8. How long does it take for you to ride a bicycle to a friend's house?

   _____
9. How long does it take to smile? _____
10. How long does it take to eat a lollipop? _____

11. How long does it take to clean your room? _____
12. How long does it take to walk to your school? _____
13. How long does it take to count to 100? _____
14. How long does it take to be ticklish? _____
15. How long does it take to take a bath? _____

Now think of some "How long does it take?" ideas of your own!

Ladybug Clock

Use the clock you make from the pieces on this page for the activites suggested on page 87.

To make the clock:

- Duplicate or mount the clock pieces on tag.
- Ask students to carefully write the numbers on the clock face in the correct positions.
- Color and cut out the clock pieces.
- Attach the hour hand and the minute hand to the center of the clock face with a brad. The minute hand should be mounted *over* the hour hand.
- Practice telling time!

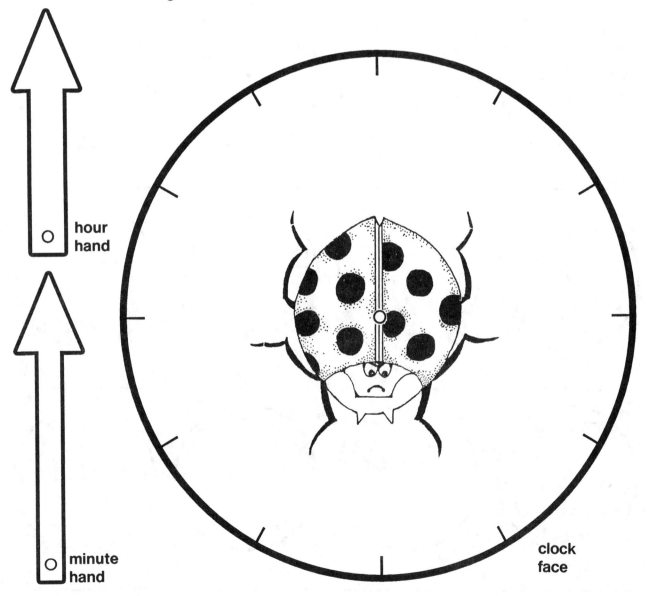

hour hand

minute hand

clock face

Do You Understand?

Show that you understood how to tell time by completing the times below correctly.

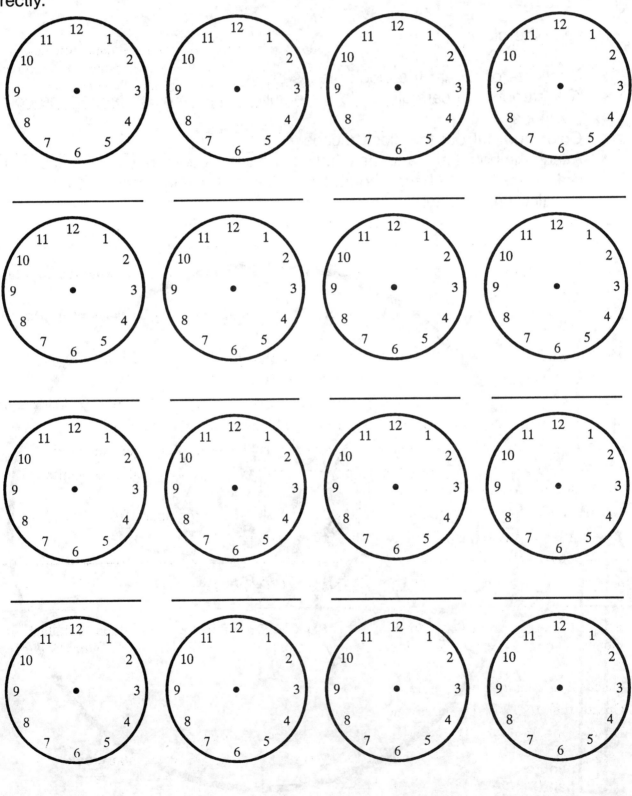

Alexander, Who Used to Be Rich Last Sunday

by Judith Viorst

Poor Alexander. His grandparents gave him one dollar when they came to visit, and now he has nothing to show for it but a deck of cards with two cards missing, a one-eyed bear, a melted candle, and bus tokens. Readers will follow his losses with interest and, perhaps recognition!

MATH CONCEPTS

- measurement • money • addition • comparison • logic • counting

---

CONNECTING ACTIVITIES

- Before reading the story, talk about the concept of rich. Ask your students what it would take to make them feel rich.
- Practice money counting skills. Use real coins or models of them, such as *Play Money*, on page 92.
- Determine what combination of coins can equal a dollar. (*The Value of Money*, page 93)
- Practice making money symbols. (*Dollars and Cents*, page 99)
- Figure the total amount of money Anthony has and the total amount of money Nicholas has.
- Keep a running tally of Alexander's financial situation as you read the story.
- Ask the students if they would spend their money in the same ways Alexander did.
- Use real money or play money to help your students grasp equal value concepts. Discuss combinations of coins that equal each other.
- Discuss and practice shopping within a budget. (*Shopping Spree!*, page 94)
- Assess concept understanding. (*Do You Understand?* page 96)

EXTENDING ACTIVITIES

- Encourage students at home to arrange real money in combinations that equal a dollar. Assign money-related homework activities, such as rolling penny rolls or *All For One Dollar!*, page 95.
- Discuss ways kids can earn money.
- Create the story of Alexander's next dollar!
- Encourage students to share money-learning experiences with the class.
- Invite a person from a bank to speak to the class about money saving plans.
- Discuss realism as it relates to the story.
- Read more Alexander books by Judith Viorst.

Play Money

Color this play money in a realistic way. Cut it out and use the money to practice your money counting skills.

92

The Value of Money

Look at the combinations of coins that can equal one dollar.

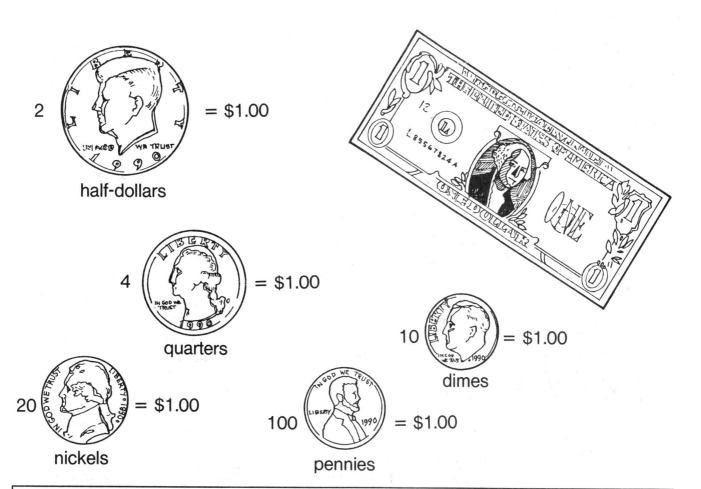

2 [half-dollar coin] = $1.00

half-dollars

4 [quarter coin] = $1.00

quarters

10 [dime coin] = $1.00

dimes

20 [nickel coin] = $1.00

nickels

100 [penny coin] = $1.00

pennies

Finish these equations. All answers must equal one dollar. Use the *Play Money* on page 92, or real money to help you.

1. ____ half-dollar + ____ quarters = $1.00

2. ____ quarters + ____ dimes = $1.00

3. ____ quarters + ____ dimes + ____ nickels = $1.00

4. ____ dimes + ____ nickels = $1.00

5. ____ dimes + ____ nickels + ____ pennies = $1.00

6. ____ nickels + ____ pennies = $1.00

7. ____ half dollar + ____ quarter + ____ dime + ____ nickel +
   ____ pennies = $1.00

Shopping Spree!

On this page you will find things you might buy and their prices. You have a dollar to spend. What would you buy on this page?

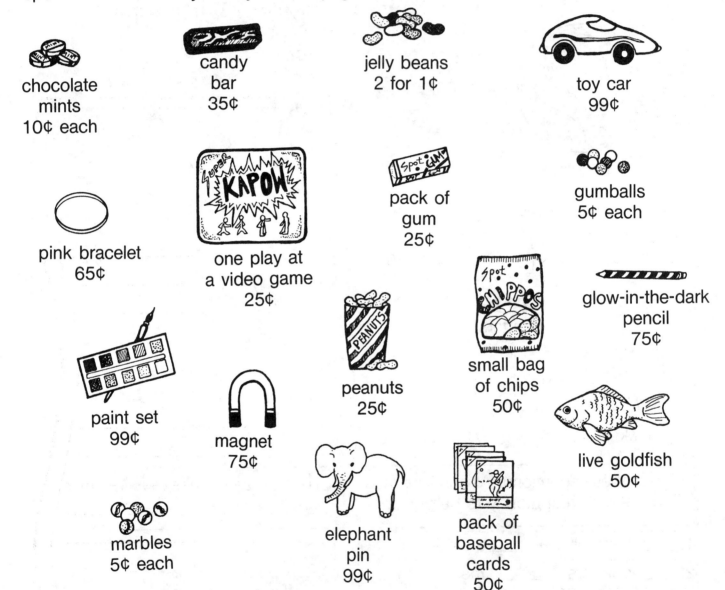

chocolate
mints
10¢ each

candy
bar
35¢

jelly beans
2 for 1¢

toy car
99¢

pink bracelet
65¢

one play at
a video game
25¢

pack of
gum
25¢

gumballs
5¢ each

paint set
99¢

magnet
75¢

peanuts
25¢

small bag
of chips
50¢

glow-in-the-dark
pencil
75¢

live goldfish
50¢

marbles
5¢ each

elephant
pin
99¢

pack of
baseball
cards
50¢

Write the things you have chosen and their prices here. Remember to add very carefully. You can't spend over a dollar!

Quantity	Item	Price	Quantity	Item	Price
_____	_____	_____	_____	_____	_____
_____	_____	_____	_____	_____	_____
_____	_____	_____	_____	_____	_____

TOTAL MONEY SPENT _____

Alexander, Who Used to Be
Rich Last Sunday

Money

All For One Dollar!

What do you think you could buy for a dollar?

With a parent or other family members, go to one or more stores
where there would be things for one dollar or less.

Make a list of the
things you could buy
for one dollar or
less. Write the
price next to each item.

Which things on your list would you
like to buy?

_____
_____
_____
_____

Which things *would* you buy if you
only had one dollar?

_____ _____
_____ _____
_____ _____
_____ _____
TOTAL SPENT $1.00

THINGS I COULD BUY WITH
ONE DOLLAR

_____ _____
_____ _____
_____
_____
_____
_____
_____
_____
_____
_____
_____
_____
_____
_____
_____

© 1991 Teacher Created Materials, Inc.

95

#342 Connecting Math and Literature

Do You Understand?

Use the words and the numbers in the box to identify the money below.

quarter	penny	dollar	1¢	5¢	$1.00
half-dollar	dime	nickel	10¢	25¢	50¢

word _____

number _____

word _____

number _____

word _____ _____ _____ _____

number _____ _____ _____ _____

Match the answers in the box below with the money equations at the bottom of the page.

65¢	$1.00	77¢	15¢	$4.00	$1.37

1. 5 pennies + 1 dime = _____
2. 1 dollar + 1 quarter + 2 nickels + 2 pennies = _____
3. 2 quarters + 2 dimes + 1 nickel + 25 pennies = _____
4. 1 half-dollar + 3 nickels = _____
5. 7 dimes + 7 pennies = _____
6. 4 quarters + 10 dimes + 20 nickels + 100 pennies = _____

Where The Sidewalk Ends

by Shel Silverstein

Shel Silverstein creates an amazing variety of poetry for *Where The Sidewalk Ends.* There is a poem for everyone in this book, including those who like to use poetry to teach math!

MATH CONCEPTS

- measurement   • money   • addition   • multiplication   • logic

---

CONNECTING ACTIVITIES

- Read "Smart." Ask students to determine exactly how much money the narrator had left by the end of the poem. (*Smart,* page 98) See if your students can tell how the father really feels about his son's money sense.

- Determine what combination of coins can equal a dollar. (*The Value of Money,* page 93)

- Practice money counting skills. Use real coins or models of them, such as the *Play Money* found on page 92.

- Introduce and practice making money symbols. (*Dollars and Cents,* page 99)

- Read "The Googies Are Coming." Arrange child prices in order of most expensive to least expensive, using *The Price of a Child,* page 100.

- Determine the cost of a bunch of children if purchased according to the googies' price list. (*Expense Account,* page 101)

- Be sure the children understand the vocabulary used in the poetry. Words such as "meek," "lean," and "husky" may need definition.

- Assess concept understanding. (*Do You Understand?,* page 102)

EXTENDING ACTIVITIES

- Ask students to pretend they are the father of the son in "Smart." They must explain the concept of what a dollar is to the boy!

- Draw pictures of what googies might look like.

- Make a new lists of children the googies have purchased. Figure out the total cost of each list of new children.

- Assign money counting homework activities, such as making penny rolls!

- Read other math-related poetry in *Where The Sidewalk Ends,* such as "Me and My Giant," "For Sale," "One Inch Tall," "Lester," and "Band-Aids."

"Smart"

In this poem a son cleverly trades his dollar to give him "more" than he started with!

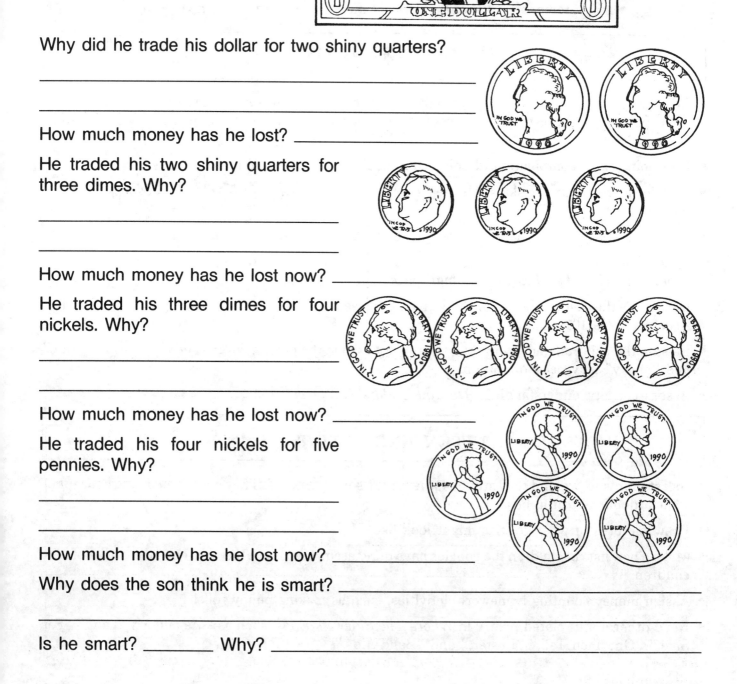

He started with
one dollar.

Why did he trade his dollar for two shiny quarters?

_____

_____

How much money has he lost? _____

He traded his two shiny quarters for
three dimes. Why?

_____

_____

How much money has he lost now? _____

He traded his three dimes for four
nickels. Why?

_____

_____

How much money has he lost now? _____

He traded his four nickels for five
pennies. Why?

_____

_____

How much money has he lost now? _____

Why does the son think he is smart? _____

_____

Is he smart? _____ Why? _____

Dollars and Cents

Practice making dollar and cent symbols.

Look at it.	Trace it.	Make it.
$	$	
Look at it.	Trace it.	Make it.
¢	¢	

Practice using dollar and cent symbols.

Read it.	Say it.	Write it.
one dollar	$1.00	
twenty-five cents	25¢	
thirteen cents	13¢	
one dollar and ten cents	$1.10	
one dollar and forty-two cents	$1.42	
seventy-six cents	76¢	
fifty-eight cents	58¢	

On the back of this sheet draw 4 toys and write the cost of each using the dollar and cent symbols.

The Price of a Child

The googies are coming to buy children and take them away. They have worked out this price list:

fat ones .... 50¢   weak ones .... 25¢

lean ones .... 20¢   noisy ones .... 1¢

dirty ones .... 15¢   meek ones $1.00

clean ones .... 30¢   happy ones .... 40¢

mean ones .... 5¢   sad ones .... 11¢

husky ones .... 80¢   bad ones .... 0¢

(They won't buy the bad ones.)

Arrange these types of children in the order of the most expensive to least expensive.

1. _____

2. _____

3. _____

4. _____

5. _____

6. _____

7. _____

8. _____

9. _____

10. _____

11. _____

12. _bad ones_ _____

How much would you cost?

_____

Expense Account

The googies have come and gone, and now have quite a few children locked up.

According to the price list that was given in the poem, how much did this group of kids cost the googies?

EXPENSE ACCOUNT: ONE BUNCH OF CHILDREN			
How Many	What Type	How Much Per Child	Total Cost
2	fat ones	50¢ each	$1.00
5	lean ones	each	
6	dirty ones	each	
1	clean ones	each	
20	mean ones	each	
1	husky ones	each	
4	weak ones	each	
78	noisy ones	each	
3	meek ones	each	
5	happy ones	each	
2	sad ones	each	
0	bad ones	0¢ each	0
		Total cost for children	

Do You Understand?

Make a dollar symbol and a cent symbol in these boxes.

dollar symbol   cent symbol

Write the following money words using numbers and symbols.

one dollar and thirty-three cents   _____

twenty-seven cents   _____

sixty-two cents   _____

one cent   _____

Would you rather have five pennies, four nickels, three dimes, two quarters, or one dollar?

_____

Why? _____

_____

If the googies bought five lean children at 20¢ each, ten mean ones at 5¢ each, and two weak ones at 25¢ each, how many children did they buy for how much money?

five lean ones = _____   Total number
                     of children = _____

ten mean ones = _____

two weak ones = _____   Total amount
                     of money spend = _____

Pattern Center

Being able to identify, repeat, and extend patterns is an important problem-solving skill. There is an abundance of great children's literature selections that can be used to teach and reinforce this problem-solving skill.

You may wish to develop a Pattern Center in your classroom that will showcase these outstanding books as well as provide a place to display other pattern-related materials. (*Sample Layout for Pattern Center,* page 104)

Here are some ideas for activities that can be done at your center:

- Supply numerous pattern books that make reading and repeating patterns fun. (*Some Great Pattern Books,* page 105) and *Bibliography,* page 142.

- Encourage math manipulatives for a hands-on approach to learning about patterns. Some types of manipulatives you may want to include are buttons, beans, unifix cubes, varieties of pasta, and pattern blocks. (Use these manipulatives with *Patterns You Can Touch!,* page 106)

- Provide different color beads and string for making pattern necklaces. Students may create their own patterns for necklaces or use *Patterns You Can Touch* for stringing ideas.

- Reproduce puzzles for pattern block pictures. An excellent source is *Pattern Animals: Puzzles for Pattern Blocks* by Sandra Mogensen and Judi Magarian-Gold. Students can select a puzzle and complete it using pattern blocks. (*Pattern Block Puzzle,* page 107)

- Supply graph paper for the students to use to create pattern designs.

- Give kids swatches of wallpaper designs. Ask them to glue the swatch on a piece of paper and extend the design to cover the entire paper. Or you may choose to create a specific pattern in the center of a page and have the students extend the pattern to fill the page. (*Finish Me!,* page 108)

- Provide color by number pattern puzzles for the children to use number recognition and operational skills to locate a pattern. (*Pattern by the Number,* pages 109 and 110)

- Give children pattern designs to create with color. (*You're the Designer!,* page 111)

- Write words of a pattern story on strips. Place all the story strips in a *Story Strip* pouch. Students will take out all the strips in a story pouch, read the words on each strip, sequence the strips in story order, and read the story to someone else in the room.

"Brown Bear, Brown Bear, What do you see?"

"I see a redbird looking at me."

- Create original pattern books. (*Animals You Can Use!,* page 112 and 113)

- Anything else you think your children would enjoy as a pattern activity!

Sample Layout for Pattern Center

Pattern Center

At this center you can:

- Select pattern books to read
- Play pattern games
- Arrange patterns
- Create your own patterns
- Sequence pattern stories
- Make your own pattern books

Graph Paper

Pattern Block Puzzles

Story Strips 1

Story Strips 2

Story Strips 3

Wallpaper Samples

Patterns by the Number

Finish Me!

Animals You Can Use!

Pattern Strips

You're the Designer!

There Was an Old Lady Who Swallowed a Fly

The Napping House

Bringing the Rain to Kapiti Plain

If You Give a Mouse a Cookie

The Rose in My Garden

Drummer Hoff

Brown Bear, Brown Bear, What Do You See?

Pasta

Beads

Unifix Cubes

Glue

Pattern Blocks

Beans

Buttons

Crayons, Markers, Pencils

Some Great Pattern Books!

Here are just a few of the many great books you will want to include in your classroom Pattern Center.

- *There Was An Old Lady Who Swallowed A Fly* illustrated by Pam Adams
  Swallowing a fly could happen in real life, but nothing else about this story is very reasonable! An old lady thinks the best way to rid herself of the fly she swallowed is to swallow a spider. However, she then needs a bird for the spider, a cat for the bird, a dog for the cat, a cow for the dog, and, finally, a horse for the cow. Children love to read and sing this funny pattern story.

- *Drummer Hoff* adapted by Barbara Emberley
  One by one, we meet all who are responsible for preparing a cannon for battle. But it is Drummer Hoff who fires it off. The last illustration in the story brings a gentle message for peace.

- *A Rose in My Garden* by Arnold Lobel
  A beautiful garden and the creatures within it are revealed to the reader in cumulative verse. *A Rose in My Garden* is a delight to look at, and a joy to read and reread.

- *Brown Bear, Brown Bear, What Do You See?* by Bill Martin, Jr.
  "What do you see?" is the question asked of each character in this story. In charming pictures and simple repetitive, rhyming text, we find out!

- *If You Give A Mouse A Cookie* by Laura Joffe Numeroff
  This enchanting and endearing story explains all that can result if you are so bold as to give a mouse a cookie. It is delightfully illustrated and easy to read, easy to memorize, and easy to enjoy!

- *Bringing the Rain to Kapiti Plain* by Verna Aardema
  The African rains usually green the great Kapiti Plain, giving food and shelter to the animals that live there. But in a year of very little rain, the Kapiti Plain began to wither and die. And, it would have, if Ki-pat the herdsman had not fashioned an arrow to shoot the great cloud overhead and bring rain to the Kapiti Plain.

- *The Napping House* by Audrey Wood
  Naptime can be a warm and cozy time. In *The Napping House*, this is the way naptime begins: One by one, a boy, a dog, a cat, and a mouse climb upon a snoring and comfortable granny to continue their rest. But an active flea quickly changes the slumbering pile!

Patterns You Can Touch!

Duplicate 15 to 20 copies of this page. Cut the pattern strips apart and place them in the *Patterns You Can Touch!* pouch on the Pattern Center board. Students will select one pattern strip from the pouch and create the pattern described on the strip using the manipulatives available at the Center. They must decide and write down the type of manipulative they have chosen to correspond with each letter of the alphabet that is on the pattern strip. When they choose another strip from the pouch to do, it must be a different one.

PATTERN STRIP #1

a = _____   b = _____
pattern to create: a a b b a a b b a a b b

PATTERN STRIP #2

a = _____   b = _____   c = _____
pattern to create: a b b c a b b c a b b c a b b c

PATTERN STRIP #3

a = _____   b = _____   c = _____
pattern to create: a b c b a b c b a b c b a b c b

PATTERN STRIP #4

a = _____   b = _____   c = _____
pattern to create: a b a c a b a c a b a c a b a c

PATTERN STRIP #5

a = _____   b = _____   c = _____   d = _____
pattern to create: a a a b c d a a a b c d a a a b c d

PATTERN STRIP #6

a = _____   b = _____   c = _____   d = _____
pattern to create: a b b a c c a d d a b b a c c a d d a

PATTERN STRIP #7

a = _____   b = _____   c = _____   d = _____
pattern to create: a b c d c b a b c d c d a b c d c b a

Have students create pattern strips for others in the class to follow!

Pattern Block Puzzle

Different combinations of pattern blocks can be used to cover the puzzle design on this page. Use any combination you would like.

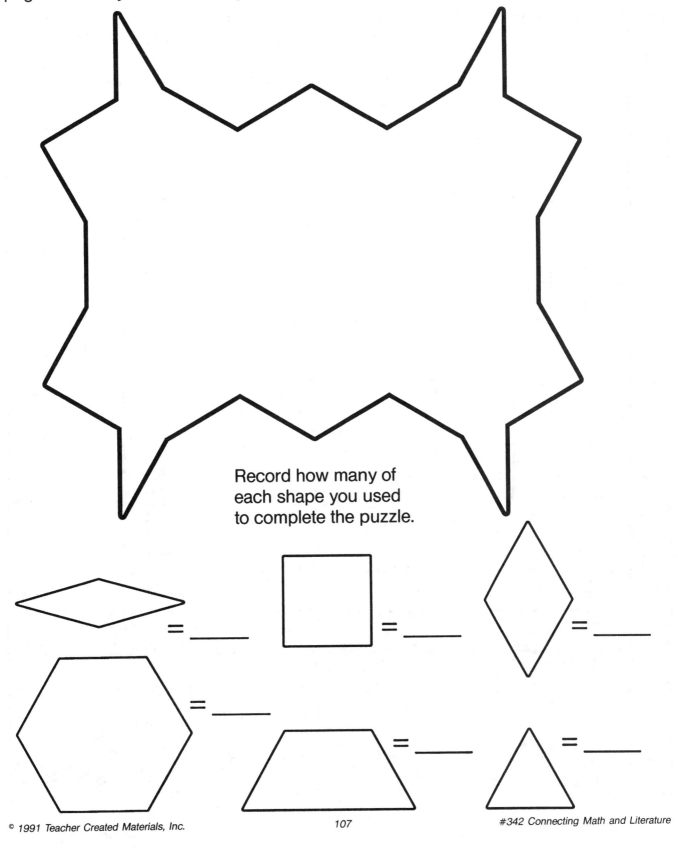

Record how many of each shape you used to complete the puzzle.

Finish Me!

Look at the color pattern in the center of this page. Continue writing this pattern until you have filled the page. Then, color it to make the pattern really come to life!

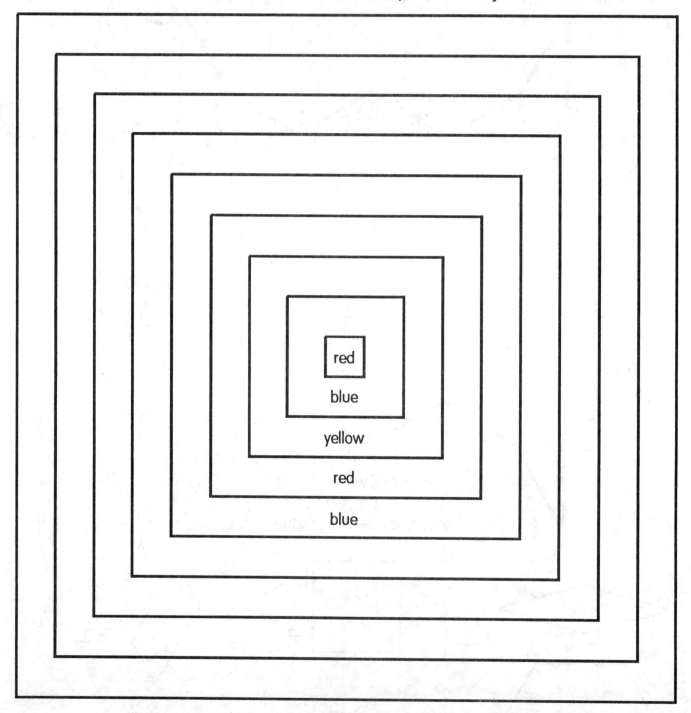

red

blue

yellow

red

blue

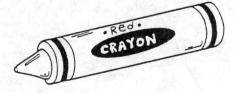

108

Pattern Center

Patterns by the Number

Use the number and color key to discover the pattern hidden on this page.

1 = Red CRAYON   2 = Blue CRAYON

3 = Yellow CRAYON   4 = Green CRAYON

5 = Orange CRAYON

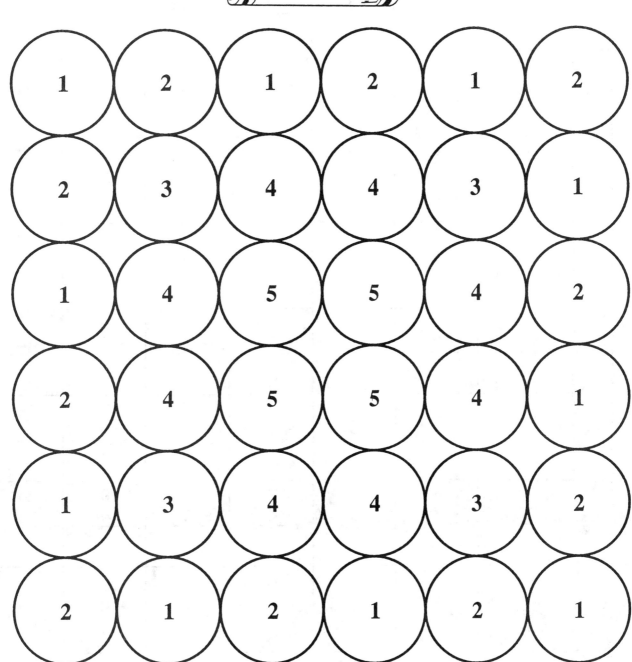

Patterns by the Number

Use your addition and subtraction skills to discover the pattern in the large square below. Color the small squares according to this key:

answers that equal 5   *Blue* CRAYON   answers that equal 7   *Yellow* CRAYON

answers that equal 6   *Red* CRAYON   answers that equal 8   *Green* CRAYON

2 + 3	1 + 6	4 + 4	3 + 3	10 - 4	10 - 2	6 + 1	12 - 7
0 + 7	1 + 4	2 + 5	9 - 1	7 + 1	5 + 2	4 + 1	7 + 0
15 - 7	10 - 3	5 + 0	3 + 4	4 + 3	8 - 3	15 - 8	8 + 0
6 + 0	6 + 2	8 - 1	6 - 1	11 - 6	9 - 2	11 - 3	12 - 6
8 - 2	10 - 2	9 - 2	3 + 2	10 - 5	4 + 3	8 - 0	2 + 4
3 + 5	11 - 4	4 + 1	2 + 5	6 + 1	7 - 2	12 - 5	12 - 4
7 + 0	15 -10	14 - 7	5 + 3	12 - 4	7 + 0	9 - 4	4 + 3
0 + 5	1 + 6	16 - 8	1 + 5	9 - 3	7 + 1	10 - 3	8 - 3

You're the Designer!

Use different colors to create your own patterns.

Animals You Can Use!

Bill Martin, Jr. used many colorful animals when he wrote his pattern book *Brown Bear, Brown Bear, What Do You See?* Color and cut out the animals on this page. Use the ones you like to help you create your own pattern book!

Animals You Can Use! (cont.)

Color and cut out the animals on this page. Use the ones you like to help you create your own pattern book!

Harriet's Halloween Candy

by Nancy Carlson

Harriet the dog collected quite an array of candy on Halloween. When she got home, she sorted it by color, size, and favorites. Then, after giving her baby brother one tiny piece she didn't like anyway, she hid it in her room. What Harriet does to try to keep the rest of her candy for herself is a method with which we might be able to identify!

MATH CONCEPTS

• problem solving   • sorting   • classification   • comparison   • counting   • sets

CONNECTING ACTIVITIES

• Dump a bag of assorted candy on a table in front of the room. Discuss the types of candy there are on the table. Brainstorm all the ways candy can be sorted. After the brainstorming session, distribute *How Many Ways?*, page 115, to the class. Talk about the various candy-sorting methods described. Practice sorting the candy on the table in some of these ways. Ask students to add their own sorting ideas at the bottom of the *How Many Ways?* page 115.

• Discuss sharing and its effects on families and friendships.

• Ask students to sort candy four ways and record their data on a chart. (*Candy Chart!,* page 116). They may use their Halloween candy, or, for those who do not celebrate Halloween or go trick-or-treating, use the *Candy Page* provided in this book. (page 117) Discuss their sorting choices in class.

• Assess concept understanding. This can easily be evidenced by the students' successful completion of the *Candy Chart* or similar in-class activities.

EXTENDING ACTIVITIES

• Encourage students to sort candy at home, recording the ways they chose to sort. Ask students to have other members of their families sort the same assortment of candy. Have them compare the ways they sorted with the ways other family members sorted.

• Have each student make a list of the things he or she shares *easily* with other family members.

• Provide a lesson in nutritious food choices.

• Provide a lesson in dental care.

• Read more Harriet books by Nancy Carlson.

114

How Many Ways?

Here are some ways to sort candy. Add some more ideas at the bottom of the page!

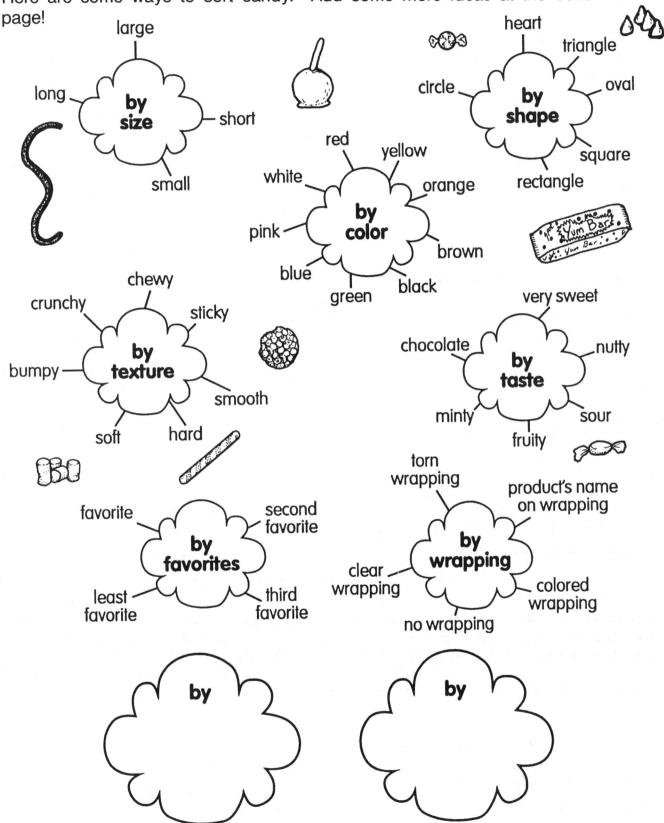

by size
- large
- long
- short
- small

by shape
- heart
- triangle
- circle
- oval
- square
- rectangle

by color
- red
- yellow
- white
- orange
- pink
- brown
- blue
- black
- green

by texture
- chewy
- crunchy
- sticky
- bumpy
- smooth
- soft
- hard

by taste
- very sweet
- chocolate
- nutty
- minty
- sour
- fruity

by favorites
- favorite
- second favorite
- least favorite
- third favorite

by wrapping
- torn wrapping
- product's name on wrapping
- clear wrapping
- colored wrapping
- no wrapping

by

by

Candy Chart!

- Sort your candy four ways. Put any candy that can't be sorted in these ways in a fifth group.
- Glue a piece of candy from each of the four groups on the chart where it is marked "Example of Candy." (You may draw a picture of it instead.)
- Write how you sorted the candy in the place on the chart marked "Ways You Sorted Your Candy."
- Count how many pieces of candy you have in each group and mark the numbers on the chart.
- Total the number of pieces of candy you have!

CANDY SORTING CHART		
Example of Candy	Ways You Sorted Your Candy	Number of Pieces
	Candy that could not be sorted in these ways	
	Total pieces of candy you have	

Candy Page

Color the candy on this page. Then sort it four ways, using the chart on page 116 to help you.

Frog and Toad Are Friends

by Arnold Lobel

In this book are five short stories about a friendship between a frog and a toad. "A Lost Button" provides an excellent springboard to a lesson in classification and graphing. In this story, Toad loses a button from his jacket. Frog and Toad look at many different kinds of buttons before the missing one is "found."

MATH CONCEPTS

- problem solving • sorting • classification • comparison • counting • sets

---

CONNECTING ACTIVITIES

- Divide the class into groups of three or four. Provide each group with a handful of buttons. Ask each group to decide how the buttons they have been given can be classified into sets. Have a spokesperson from each group report storing methods his or her group used.

- Distribute *Bunches of Buttons!*, page 119, and *The Button Graph*, page 120, to the class. Ask students to classify and graph these buttons.

- Dramatize "A Lost Button" in class, with children playing the parts of the narrator, Toad, Frog, a sparrow, a raccoon, and, if you choose, the buttons!

- Assess concept understanding. Successful group classification involvement and the completion of *The Button Graph* would indicate concept mastery. If further evaluation is needed, ask each student to classify a handful of buttons for you!

EXTENDING ACTIVITIES

- Read and discuss the other stories in *Frog and Toad Are Friend.* Arnold Lobel has written other *Frog and Toad* books your students would enjoy, too!

- Go for a walk. Look for buttons!

- Talk about the giving of very special gifts. Make a gift list of special things you could give your family and best friends.

- Learn how to sew a button on a piece of cloth.

- Sort all the buttons in the family sewing box!

Bunches of Buttons!

Classify the buttons on this page by using the ways of sorting written on *The Button Graph*, page 120. Buttons may be used in more than one of these classficiations. Then, graph your data on *The Button Graph*.

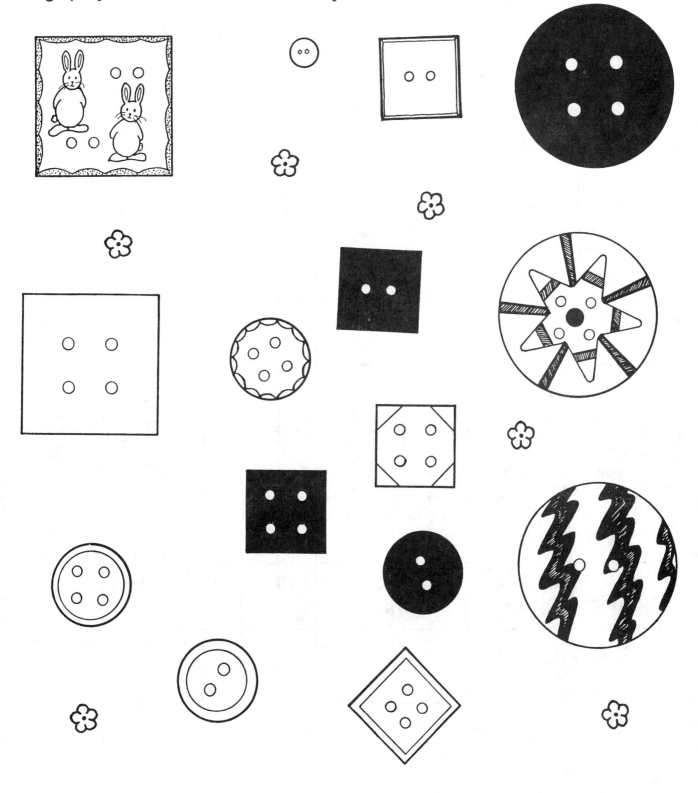

The Button Graph

Record your data from *Bunches of Buttons*, page 119, by coloring in the bars on this graph. Remember, buttons may be used in more than one classification.

BUNCHES OF BUTTONS BAR GRAPH

number of buttons

ways to sort buttons	0	1	2	3	4	5	6	7
all white with two holes								
all white with four holes								
all black with two holes								
all black with four holes								
small								
big								
round, any color, with two holes								
round, any color, with four holes								
square, any color, with two holes								
square, any color, with four holes								

A House Is a House for Me

by Mary Ann Hoberman

In this delightful rhyming book, houses and their owners are identified. After reading this book, children will look at the world around them in an entirely different way!

MATH CONCEPTS

- problem solving • classification • logic • sets

CONNECTING ACTIVITIES

- Bring in an assortment of things that can "house" other things. (Be sure to include items that require some critical thinking skills to determine "ownership.") Ask your students to give ideas as to who or what could live in these houses.

- Brainstorm for ideas of the types of things that could be houses for children. Ask the students to name things that could never serve as houses for them as well.

- Prepare a choral reading of this story, giving each child a part to read or memorize. Perform the story for an audience!

- Practice matching houses and their owners. (*Find Me A Home!*, page 122 and 123, and *Who Owns This House?*, page 124)

- Assess concept understanding by observing students as they write about and discuss houses and their owners.

EXTENDING ACTIVITIES

- Make displays of some of the houses mentioned in the story.

- Ask your students to write a story as if they were one of the owners living in one of the houses in *A House Is a House for Me*.

- Encourage students to explore the types of houses they can find for themselves in their own homes and yards. Ask them to share, physically or verbally, what they have discovered!

- Research different types of houses that are used by people in different places in the world.

- Study animal homes.

- Ask students to build a bird's nest out of building materials such as sticks, leaves, yarn, etc.

- Ask your students to draw a picture of what they think their home will look like fifty years from now.

- Encourage students to write their own lists of "A(n) _____ is a house for a(n) _____ ." Share all ideas with the class.

Find Me A Home!

Color these home owners and cut them out. Then, match them with their homes on page 123.

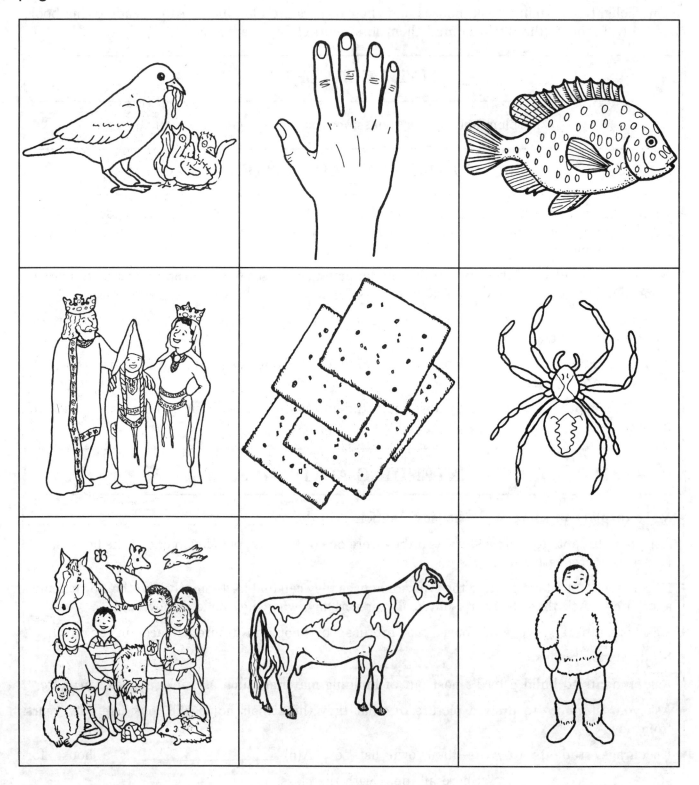

Find Me A Home! (continued)

Color these homes and cut them out. Then, match them with their owners on page 122.

Who Owns This House?

The houses and their owners are all listed on this page. They are just a little mixed-up!

Match each house with its owner.

1. _____ teacup   a. banana
2. _____ book   b. feet
3. _____ stapler   c. ink
4. _____ banana peel   d. pillow
5. _____ swimming pool   e. money
6. _____ plate   f. staples
7. _____ tree   g. sand
8. _____ aquarium   h. ice cream
9. _____ pen   i. Indian
10. _____ cone   j. tea
11. _____ bank   k. ring
12. _____ toaster   l. butterfly
13. _____ finger   m. water
14. _____ sandbox   n. students
15. _____ tepee   o. toast
16. _____ bed   p. leaves
17. _____ classroom   q. words
18. _____ shell   r. fish
19. _____ cocoon   s. crab
20. _____ shoes   t. dinner

124

Q is for Duck

by Mary Elting and Michael Folsom

In this unusual alphabet book, readers are given the chance to guess why the authors have selected animals for certain letters. Q is for Duck? Of course, because a duck quacks! There are twenty-five more of these to guess!

MATH CONCEPTS

• problem solving • characteristics • logic • comparison

CONNECTING ACTIVITIES

• Read *Q is for Duck* very slowly with the class. After each alphabet question, give the chance for all class members to respond. Write the responses on the board. Then, compare the answers the students gave with those of the authors. Read the whole book like this, page by page. The students love to try to guess the answers the authors gave! Be sure to discuss the fact that there can be more than one right answer.

• Assign each class member a letter of the alphabet. They are to memorize their part in *Q is for Duck* and, as a group, perform the book for an audience.

• Encourage students to make their own guessing game alphabet books. They must use all twenty-six letters. The book can be made by individuals, in groups, in families, or as a class. One page to help get started is in this book. (*Here Come The Animals!*, page 126)

• Discuss why the choices the authors made work. Discuss logical thinking.

• Assess concept understanding. (*Do You Understand?*, page 127)

EXTENDING ACTIVITIES

• Discuss the characteristics of animals and how knowing these characteristics can help a reader solve the questions in *Q is for Duck*, or write their own guessing game books.

• Play games of "twenty questions" related to animals and their characteristics. All questions in the game must relate to size, color, food choices, habitat, or be other characteristic-oriented questions.

• Observe animals. List the characteristics they exhibit.

• Share *Q is for Duck* with someone who has not read it. Is the new reader a logical thinker?

Here Come The Animals!

Color and cut out the animals on this page. Use them to make your own guessing game alphabet book!

_____ is for Dragon.

Why?

_____ is for Mouse.

Why?

_____ is for Turtle.

Why?

_____ is for Monkey.

Why?

Do You Understand?

Look at the animal pictures in the boxes below. Then, answer each question.

P is for Kangaroo.

Why?
Because a Kangaroo

_____

S is for Zebra.

Why?
Because a Zebra

_____

H is for Unicorn.

Why?
Because a Unicorn

_____

G is for Bear.

Why?
Because a Bear

_____

Logic

Ming Lo Moves the Mountain
by Arnold Lobel

Nestled at the base of a tall mountain is the little house of Ming Lo and his wife. But, they are not happy in the shadow of the mountain. Ming Lo decides to move the mountain away from the house and seeks the counsel of the wise man in the village. In this story, logic is left behind as Ming Lo and his wife, in their own amazing way, succeed in moving the mountain. Readers will delight in knowing something the characters in the story do not!

MATH CONCEPTS

- problem solving   - logic   - comparison   - measurement   - classification

CONNECTING ACTIVITIES

- Pose this question to your students before reading the story: "If you love your house but not where you live, what would you do?"
- Ask your students why they think Ming Lo and his wife did not know the truth, and the wise man did not tell the truth.
- Brainstorm for ways Ming Lo and his wife could have made a living under the shadow of the mountain more bearable.
- Ask students to demonstrate "the dance of the moving mountain."
- Discuss the importance of logic in everyday decision making.
- Introduce word problems that require logical thinking in order to arrive at answers. (*It's Logical!*, page 129)
- Create dialogues between characters in the story. For example, students could write a dialogue that might have occurred between Ming Lo, his wife, and the neighbors who saw them walking backwards carrying all their possessions. They could also write what the wise man said to others about Ming Lo's belief in mountain moving. Another dialogue idea is explained in *You Want The Truth?* on page 130.
- Assess concept understanding. (*Do You Understand?*, page 131)

EXTENDING ACTIVITIES

- Collect examples of logical and illogical stories, songs, and poems. Compare Ming Lo and his wife with other characters in literature.
- In a safe place, with someone else overseeing your safety, walk backwards doing the "dance of the moving mountain." Keep your eyes closed!
- Ask students to make lists of logical and illogical behavior they see at school, at home, in the neighborhood, or on television.
- Do your students perceive themselves as logical thinkers? Ask them why.

It's Logical!

Ming Lo and his wife have a hard time separating what could logically happen in their world and what could not. Can you separate what is logical from what is not?

Circle the things on this list that you think are logical and could happen. Cross out those things you think are not logical and would probably never happen. Be ready to explain your choices.

1. Your teacher gives a million dollars to each student in the room, including you.

2. You move a very large mountain using a cut tree.

3. You get a new bicycle for your tenth birthday.

4. If you squeeze it correctly, you can make a quarter look like a penny.

5. Your entire class has had perfect attendance all year.

6. The pencil you are writing with will write forever.

7. If Matt sat on your right side and Katie sat on your left side, Matt and Katie could not be sitting side by side.

8. Ten pennies, two nickels and one dime are all worth the same amount of money.

9. If you need light, and all you have is a candle and a match, a match is more important.

10. If you had ten apples and you ate two, you would have eight apples left.

You Want The Truth?

Ming Lo has come into the village to thank the wise man for teaching him the dance of the moving mountain. But, the wise man has decided to tell Ming Lo the truth.

Color these pictures. Then write the words Ming Lo and the wise man might say to each other if the truth was to be told.

Do You Understand?

Color the picture that shows how Ming Lo's house was moved from the base of the mountain. Then, at the bottom of the page, explain what really happened.

_____

_____

_____

The Secret Birthday Message
by Eric Carle

On the eve of his birthday, Tim discovers that an envelope has been tucked under his pillow. In it is a secret message that uses shapes to give him directions for finding his birthday present!

MATH CONCEPTS

- sequence • geometry • comparison

CONNECTING ACTIVITIES

- Introduce the shapes used in *The Secret Birthday Message.*
- Find geometrical shapes in your classroom, such as a square closet, a circular clock, a rectangular door, an oval sink, etc.
- Make shape stencils. (*Stencils,* page 133)
- Ask students to write or verbalize the directions Tim will need to take to retrace his steps back to his bedroom.
- Use stencils and other materials to create student-made, cut-out, shape books.
- Encourage students to write their own secret messages using shapes to give directions.
- Assess concept understanding. (*Do You Understand?,* page 137)

EXTENDING ACTIVITIES

- Make geometrically-shaped cookies. Before they are eaten, each shape must be correctly identified.
- Find geometrical shapes in nature. (*Shape Hunt!,* pages 134, 135, 136) Share the information with the class.
- Read *Circles, Triangles, and Squares* by Tana Hoban and *Listen To A Shape* by Marcia Brown. See shapes they have found in everyday things.
- Ask students to go on a shape hunt in one or more rooms of their houses. They are to look for and report on matches between shapes they have learned and things in their homes.
- Discuss special presents students have received for birthdays and other occasions.
- Encourage students to ask and answer story-related higher level thinking questions such as these:
  1. Did Tim have fun hunting for his birthday present? Would you if you were Tim?
  2. Did Tim go back to his bedroom the same way he came? Why?
  3. Who gave Tim the present? What are some clues from the story that support your choice?

Stencils

Use tagboard or other heavy paper to make stencil patterns or shapes. These stencils can be used to make your own shape books!

Use a shape pattern
to draw the outline
of a shape on tag.

Cut the shape out of
the tag.

Use your
stencil pattern
to draw the
shape you have
cut out!

Shape Hunt!

1. Color this *Shape Hunt Scope* cover.

2. Cut out the cover and paste it over a paper towel roll.

3. Attach the large shape circles (pages 135 and 136) one at a time to the end of the scope with a rubber band.

4. Use this scope to hunt for each shape you see when you look at things through your scope.

5. Keep a record of your findings!

Shape Hunt Scope

My name: _____

Shape Hunt! (cont.)

Use these shape circles with your *Shape Hunt Scope* to go on a shape hunt!

1. Cut out each of these four large circles.
2. Cut out the area inside each shape marked "cut out." (Parent volunteers can help students with this part, if necessary.)
3. Attach the large circles to the *Shape Hunt Scope* with a rubber band.
4. Go on a shape hunt and record your findings!

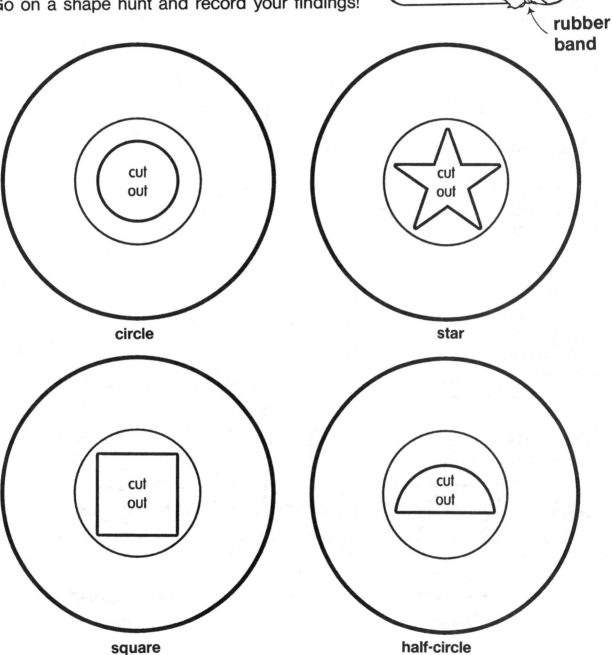

circle

star

square

half-circle

Shape Hunt! (cont.)

Use these shape circles with your *Shape Hunt Scope* to go on a shape hunt! Assemble according to directions on page 135.

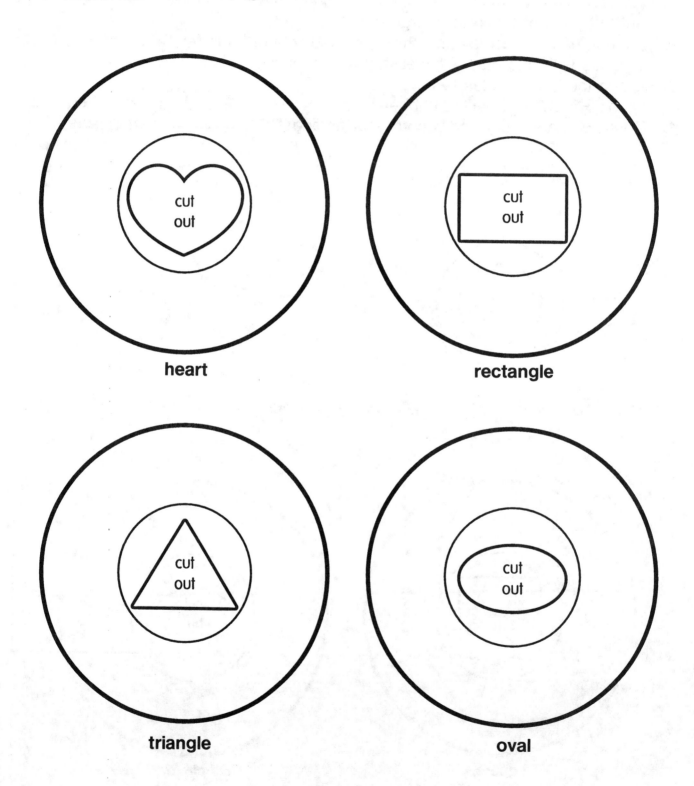

Do You Understand?

Use the words in the wordbox to name each shape below.

heart	square	circle	oval
triangle	rectangle	star	half-circle (or semi-circle)

Grandfather Tang's Story

by Ann Tompert

Little Soo and her grandfather sat under the peach tree in their backyard making different shapes with tangram puzzles. She asked him to tell her a story about the fox fairies, Chou and Wu Ling, who were able to change their shapes. Grandfather Tang used tangrams to tell his story, arranging the tans to show the different animals the fox fairies become.

MATH CONCEPTS

- capacity   - classification   - comparison   - geometry

CONNECTING ACTIVITIES

- Introduce tangrams. An excellent explanation can be found on the last page of *Grandfather Tang's Story*.
- Provide students with small and large tangram puzzle patterns which they will cut into parts. They must keep the small puzzle pieces separate from the large puzzle pieces. (*Tangrams*, page 139)
- Students can compare and classify the pieces of one puzzle according to size and shape. Introduce *triangle, square,* and *rhomboid*.
- Ask them to put the pieces of one puzzle back into a square.
- Encourage students to manipulate the tans to make different things. Remind them that all tans must be used in the design, and must be touching, but not overlapping.
- Ask students to use their own tangram puzzles to create the animal tangrams used in *Grandfather Tang's Story*.
- Use tangrams to tell stories you and the students have created.
- Provide outlines of things that can be made with tangrams. (*Can You Make These Animals?*, page 140) Encourage students to make their own tangram outlines to trade with their classmates and fill with tans.
- Assess concept understanding. (*Do You Understand?*, page 141)

EXTENDING ACTIVITIES

- Make a bulletin board display of tangrams students have created and glued on colorful paper.
- Practice *origami;* the art of paper folding.
- Send a tangram puzzle home with each child. The homework assignment is to explain tangrams to a parent, construct a tangram for that parent, and draw an outline of a tangram the parent creates! The parent tangram outlines can be shared the next day in class.
- Use pattern blocks to create tangram-like animals and other shapes. A good source book for this activity is *Pattern Animals: Puzzles for Pattern Blocks* by Sandra Mogensen and Judi Magarian-Gold. (Cuisenaire Company, 1986)

Tangrams

Use these tangrams
for the activities
described on page
138.

small
tangram
puzzle

large tangram puzzle

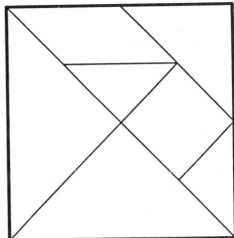

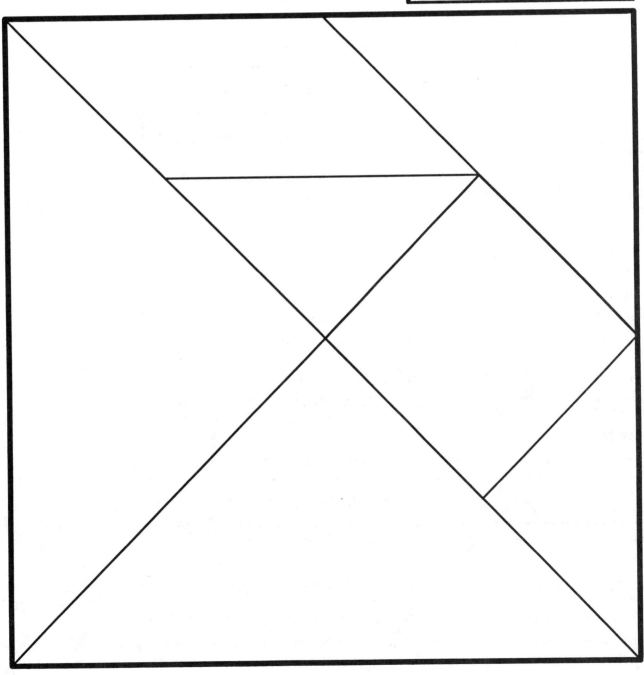

Can You Make These Animals?

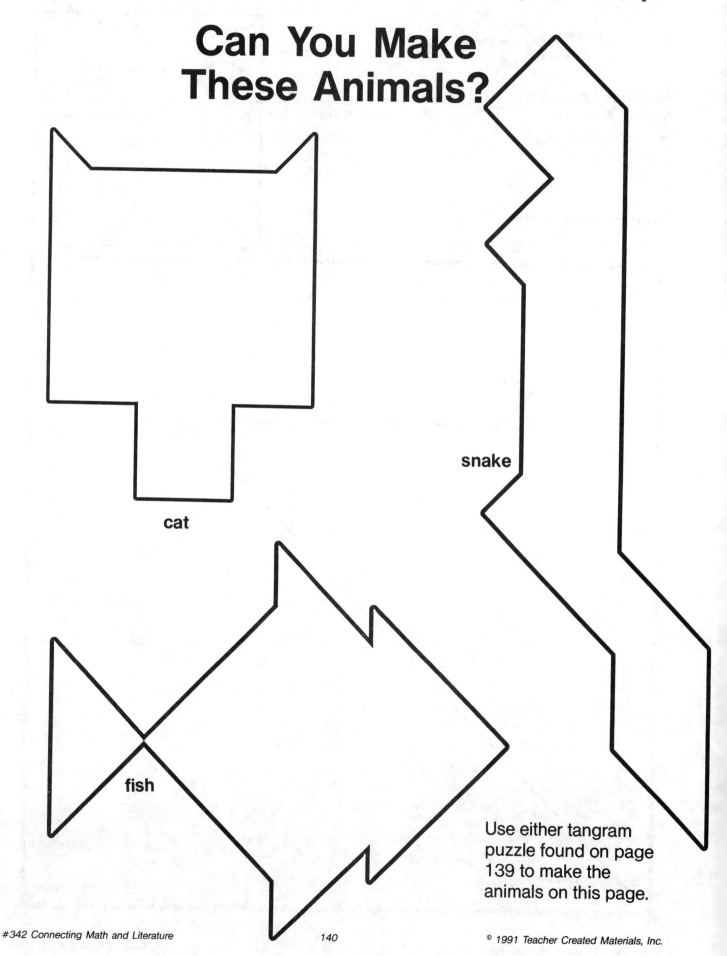

cat

snake

fish

Use either tangram puzzle found on page 139 to make the animals on this page.

Do You Understand?

Color the squares that have been cut into tangrams.

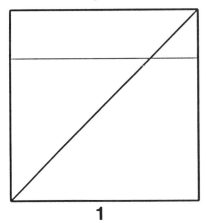

1

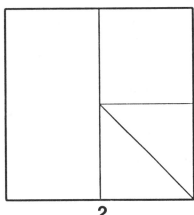

2

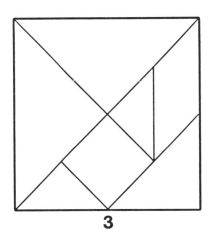

3

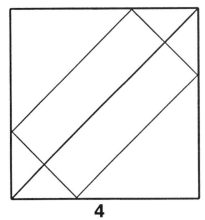

4

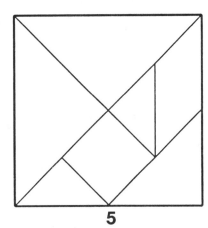

5

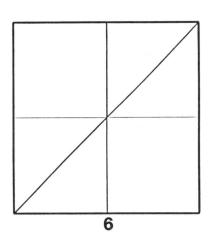

6

In a tangram, a square is divided into _____ pieces. These are the shapes you fill find in a tangram:

_____ large triangle(s)   _____ square(s)

_____ medium triangle(s)   _____ rhomboid(s)

_____ small triangle(s)

Name four animals you have made with tangrams.

_____   _____

_____   _____

Bibliography

Here are some additional titles to add to your *Connecting Math and Literature* library.

Anno, Mitsumasa. *Anno's Counting House* (Philomel, 1982)
  Anno's Math Games (Philomel, 1987)
  Anno's Mysterious Multiplying Jar (Philomel, 1983)

Asch, Frank. *Popcorn* (Parents' Magazine Press, 1979)

Bang, Molly. *Ten, Nine, Eight.* (Greenwillow, 1983)

Brown, Marcia. *Listen To A Shape* (Franklin Watts, 1979)

Bowers, Kathleen Rice. *At This Very Minute.* (Little, 1983)

Chalmers, Mary. *Six Dogs, Twenty-Three Cats, Forty-Five Mice, and One Hundred Sixteen Spiders* (Harper & Row, 1986)

Douglass, Barbara. *The Chocolate Chip Cookie Contest* (Lothrop, Lee & Shepard, 1985)

Feelings, Muriel. *Moja Means One: Swahili Counting Book* (Dial, 1971)

Gag, Wanda. *Millions of Cats.* (Coward-McCann, 1988)

Hoban, Tana. *Circles, Triangles, and Squares* (Macmillan, 1974)
  Is It Larger? Is It Smaller? (Greenwillow, 1985)

Keats, Ezra Jack. *Apt. 3* (Aladdin, 1986)

Lopshire, Robert. *The Biggest, Smallest, Fastest, Tallest Things You've Ever Heard Of* (Crowell, 1980)

Mosel, Arlene. *The Funny Little Woman* (E.P. Dutton, 1986)

Seuss, Dr. *The 500 Hats of Bartholomew Cubbins* (Vanguard, 1965)

Slobodkina, Esphyr. *Caps For Sale* (Harper & Row, 1987)

Stenmark, Jean Kerr, Virginia Thompson, and Ruth Cossey. *Family Math* (University of California, 1986)

Answer Key

p. 24   Birds, apples, shoes, and butterflies are sets. Accept all reasonable explanations.

p. 26   32 hearts, 12 ice cream cones, 25 stars, 18 pencils, 13 caterpillars = 100

p. 32   1) d 2) g 3) b 4) e 5) a 6) h 7) c 8) f
Stars, fish, sand grains, and people on our planet could be measured in millions.

p. 36   pencils and erasers, caterpillars and butterflies, shoes and hats

p. 39   1) 1 butterfly 2) 3 apples 3) 2 skateboards 4) 1 marble 5) 2 books 6) 2 horses

p. 49   a) 7 b) 2 c) 8 d) 12 e) 15
color d

p. 51   1+11, 2+10, 3+9, 4+8, 5+7, 6+6, 7+5, 8+4, 9+3, 10+2, 11+1

p. 54   ÷, 2=6 each, 4=3 each, 6=2 each, 12=1 each

p. 57   1) in fourths 2) in eighths 3) in sixths 4) in eighths 5) 25 pizzas in eighths or 50 pizzas in fourths!

p. 61   greater than: 2, 6, 9, 11, 16, 17, 18, 23, 24, 25, 28, 30
less than: 1, 3, 5, 7, 12, 15, 20, 21, 27
equal to: 4, 8, 10, 13, 14, 19, 22, 26, 29

p. 64   1) Joey 2) Eddie 3) Pete, Tami 4) Eddie 5) Sue's 6) Sue

p. 66   Accept reasonable answers.

p. 68   pencil, dominoes, peanuts, toothbrush, paperclips, pennies,
The first inchworm is an inch long.

pages 76, 77   winter: snowman, snowcap, sled
spring: baby birds ..., a green sprout ..., budding flowers
summer: plum ..., swimming pool, hot weather
autumn: Jack-o-lantern, squirrel ..., falling leaves

p. 78   spring: green buds, warm rain, tiny shoot, fragrant
summer: purple plum, blasts, sizzle, blazing
autumn: acorns, harvest, gold pumpkins, yellow leaves
winter: ice crystals, freezing, snowflake, blizzard

p. 79   winter (no bathing suit)
spring (all pictures)
summer (no mittens)
autumn (all pictures),

p. 82

```
W S D E C E M B E R B E T S A E
D S A A U H W D R E N S E G Y J
D E Z G H G S E T J P H G B V A
F G X K J F E B R U A R Y M F N
V N Q I W K H U L N P O P K E U
M M A Y S G T S E R N B O S A
U W A B P Z C S Z K I C M A G R
A Z R H L A A E Q D L A J U L Y
Q A C J Y B P P A Z D Z E G O D
Z W H P V O C T O B E R G U P J
S X T W C J D E K E U I F S L H
E D J N O V E M B E R T S T K T
C R G E A D H B E Y Q E P E J E
F V F Q X S J E W U J S K W U Q
T E C Z E W L R R I P C L Q T E
```

winter: December, January, February
spring: March, April, May
summer: June, July, August
autumn: September, October, November
1) c 2) f 3) b 4) d 5) a 6) e 7) h 8) g

p. 85   1) d 2) a 3) c 4) f 5) b 6) g 7) e

p. 88   Accept reasonable answers.

p. 93   Accept any correct combination of coins.

p. 96   1) 15¢ 2) $1.37 3) $1.00 4) 65¢ 5) 77¢ 6) $4.00

p. 98
- 2 is more than 1 — 50¢
- 3 is more than 2 — 70¢
- 4 is more than 3 — 80¢
- 5 is more than 4 — 95¢

p. 100   meek, husky, fat, happy, clean, weak, lean, dirty, sad, mean, noisy, bad

p. 101   fat: $1.00
lean: $1.00
dirty: 90¢
clean: 30¢
mean: $1.00
husky: 80¢
weak: $1.00
noisy: 78¢
meek: $3.00
happy: $2.00
sad: 22¢
bad: 0
TOTAL: $12.00

p. 102 $1.00 (5) + 50¢ (10) + 50¢ (2)
17 children for $2.00

Answer Key (continued)

p. 107

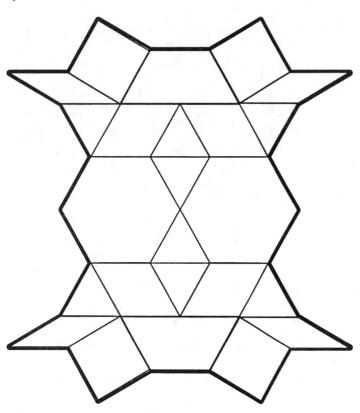

p. 120   white 2 : 3
white 4 : 5
black 2 : 2
black 4 : 2

small : 7
big : 5

round 2 : 4
round 4 : 4
square 2 : 2
square 4 : 5

p. 124   1) j 2) q 3) f 4) a 5) m 6) t 7) p 8) r 9) c
10) h 11) e 12) o 13) k 14) g 15) i 16) d
17) n 18) s 19) l 20) b

p. 127   Accept reasonable answers.

p. 129   Accept logical answers and explanations.

p. 131   Ming Lo and his wife dismantled the
house and carried it away from the
mountain.

p. 140

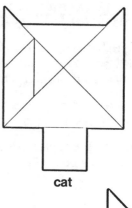

cat

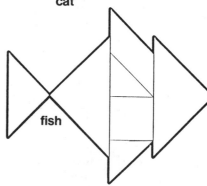

fish

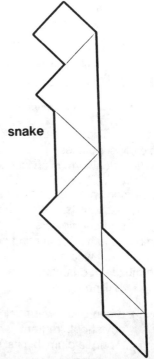

snake

p. 141   7 pieces:
2 large triangles, 1 medium triangle,
2 small triangles, 1 square, 1 rhomboid
color #'s 3 and 5